D1004848

THE ART OF

QUESTIONING

Peter Megargee Brown

The Art of Questioning

THIRTY MAXIMS OF CROSS-EXAMINATION

Macmillan Publishing Company
New York
Collier Macmillan Publishers
London

Macmillan Publishing Company
886 Third Avenue, New York, NY 10022
Collier Macmillan Canada, Inc.

Library of Congress Cataloging-in-Publication Data
Brown, Peter M. (Peter Megargee)
The art of questioning.
Includes index.
1. Cross-examination – United States.
I. Title.
KF8920.B76 1987 347.73'75 86-18264
347.30775

ISBN 0-02-517450-9

Macmillan books are available at special discounts for bulk purchases for sales promotions, premiums, fund-raising, or educational use.
For details contact:

Special Sales Director
Macmillan Publishing Company
866 Third Avenue
New York, NY 10022

10 9 8 7 6 5 4

Designed by Jack Meserole

Printed in the United States of America

To the memory of

JOHN MARSHALL HARLAN

CONTENTS

AUTHOR'S PROLOGUE

Asking the right question is 50 percent of the answer. "A prudent question," Sir Francis Bacon said, "is one-half of wisdom. . . . He that questions much learns much." Not many of us realize how important questions are or how to form them.

Consider, for example, this exchange at the Reagan White House which transpired between harassed White House spokesman Larry Speakes and two questioning members of the White House press corps. The topic was how the White House, through Mr. Speakes, handled the news about President Reagan's skin cancer. Initially, Mr. Speakes refused to confirm that a biopsy was performed to determine whether the president's pimple was cancerous. Not until a week later (after numerous media speculations) did the president himself confirm the reports.

The official White House transcript reveals the needling thrust of out-of-court questioning:

SAM DONALDSON (of ABC News): [*to Speakes*] Wait a moment. You were asked last Thursday . . . whether a biopsy would be performed, and you said, "Sure," well then you were saying one was going to be performed.

SPEAKES: Well?

HELEN THOMAS (of UPI): And on Friday you refused to say one was performed.

SPEAKES: That's right. But refusal to say does not constitute a lie, Helen.

THOMAS: Well, we are questioning your candor.

SPEAKES: No. No.

THOMAS: You were not candid.

SPEAKES: I was. I told the truth. And I told the truth from the first.

THOMAS: Well, on Friday were you candid when—

SPEAKES: Do you want to say that I did not tell the truth?

THOMAS: Aw, come on, get off of that.

SPEAKES: No, you come on. You've accused me of something.

THOMAS: You pulled an iron curtain down on the truth.

SPEAKES: Exactly right. But I did not lie. And I told the truth.

THOMAS: Is it exactly right that you did?

SPEAKES: I told the truth. Now, let's go back to yours.

DONALDSON: [*cherishing Helen Thomas's metaphor*] Well, what's the difference between pulling down an iron curtain on the truth, and being completely credible, or not being completely credible? Do you see any difference in those?

SPEAKES: I'm completely credible. I told the truth from top to bottom. And if you'll look at it you will see. Now, I think you ought to clarify the record as to what you said here. Would you like to do that? I think you owe an obligation. When you raise an accusation like that . . .

DONALDSON: I'm not withdrawing a thing about questions being raised about your credibility.

SPEAKES: [*voice rising*] All right, what are the questions? What are the questions? Raise the questions!

When Jimmy Carter retired from the presidency, he said that two things he had no trouble bequeathing to

Ronald Reagan were Menachem Begin and Sam Donaldson.

One might ask, was it much ado about nothing? After all, it is probably only in America where questions about a president's skin problem can cause a furor. But this particular incident symbolizes the importance of questions to our republican way of life. If we cannot ask questions about a skin problem, how can we expect to ask questions about MX missiles, budget deficits, and tax reforms? And the same is true for corporate board meetings, co-op apartment meetings, or PTA meetings. Knowing how to *form* the right question is the powerful weapon in our society.

Former White House counsel Fred Fielding is a wise and incisive questioner. When President Reagan was under anesthesia in the course of colon surgery, delicate determination had to be made of when the president was free of the drug's effects and back in control of his full executive powers. *The New York Times* reported that Fred Fielding looked the president in the eye and asked a single question: "Where's the rest of you?" The president instantly responded with a broad grin and let those gathered at his bedside know that he appreciated this allusion to his 1965 autobiography, *Where's the Rest of Me?*

Another sample: posted in a booth at the venerable New York Stock Exchange on Wall Street recently was this message about questions:

Answers: $1.00
Answers which require thought: $2.00
Correct answers: $4.00
Dumb looks are still free.

At Broadway's famous Lindy's Restaurant, a customer asked a waiter, "What time is it?"

THE WAITER: Sorry, sir, but this is not my table.

Sometimes a person can field an unfair or irrelevant question by lobbing back a dynamite self-serving answer. Last summer, a motorcyclist was arrested in Oxford, England, for speeding. The lady prosecutor bore in on the defendant with a curved question: "Mr. Setright, your motorcycle is capable, is it not, of exceeding the 70 mph speed limit?" He answered,

> Certainly it can exceed that limit. But the possibilities implicit in that physical ability are irrelevant to these proceedings. We are not here to consider what I might have been doing, but for the prosecution to prove, if they can, that I was doing what they allege I was doing. Were it otherwise you might just as well be here accusing me of rape, simply on the grounds that I have the necessary apparatus.

Jolted by this incisive and curiously metaphoric response, the three magistrates turned their attention to acquittal, as reported by the accused in *Cycle Guide*, conveyed by *Forbes*.

Never be afraid to ask dumb questions, even if you do not know the subject, but always, please, do so only when *outside* the courtroom.

But sometimes a dumb question can illuminate the day. The great philanthropist and art collector Paul Mellon was working in his Virginia farmhouse library. In the hallway he had hung a painting by Vincent van Gogh. His granddaughter came into the house with a young school chum. The friend stopped in the hall to look at the van Gogh painting. To his consternation, Paul Mellon heard her ask, "Who paints?"

A nighttime radio and television interviewer, "Master of the Mike" Larry King, has acquired fame for his questioning technique with a variety of guests, such as the negotiator Herb Cohen, about the hostage crisis in Lebanon. According to *Time,* King provides "a refreshing strain of intelligent, graceful conversation." King says, "The best interviewers are those who know the least about a subject. I hate to ask questions I know the answers to, and I've never been afraid to ask what might be a dumb question."

Keep in mind that all questions need not be dead serious. We deserve some fun in life. For example, the old burlesque king Minsky used to delight his audience with this question:

> Why are fire engines painted red? I'll tell ya. Fire engines are painted red because newspapers are read, too. Two and two is four. Four and four is eight. Eight and four is twelve. Twelve inches is a ruler. Queen Mary was a ruler. *Queen Mary* was a ship that sailed the sea. There are fish in the sea. The fish have fins. The Finns fought the Russians. The Russians are red. Fire engines are always rushin'. That's why fire engines are red.

Thomas Griffin tells of the affectation of the editor of the old *New York Tribune,* Horace Greeley, to pluralize as the English do when a singular word has a plural context, as in "the government are concerned." One day Greeley impatiently cabled this question to one of his overseas correspondents, "Are there any news?" The answer was cabled back to Greeley, "Sorry, not a single new."

Try to formulate and, if you can, write down your question. Keep it short and hone your inquiry. Leave out elliptical clauses, qualifying phrases, asides, irrelevancies, jokes, and historical quotes and references. Go for the jugular. At the least, review your questions two or three times in your head including your emphasis. Thomas E. Dewey would whip out a pencil and sketch his thrust. Some, such as Whitney North Seymour, Sr., would write down one or two words if technical or complex. Winston Churchill never spoke or questioned without having committed the words to memory after the keenest sculpturing. Let's face it, a badly formed and badly toned question never gets an answer worth a damn.

There's a story my partner tells about Calvin Coolidge. In 1924 President Coolidge telephoned his Amherst classmate Harlan Fiske Stone at Columbia Law School where he was the dean, to come down to the White House for breakfast. Coolidge had previously asked Stone if he would be interested in being appointed attorney general and Stone had declined. Coolidge and Stone sat in silence at the breakfast for some time, when suddenly Coolidge said: "I sent your name to the Senate." Harlan Fiske Stone, after a moment, said, "Thank you." As Stone left the White House he asked the guard at the entrance booth, "Excuse me, young man, but would you please tell me where is the Department of Justice?"

Cross-examination—whether in the courtroom or the boardroom or the classroom—is the keenest test of truth and more penetrating than an affidavit. Sharpening your skills in questioning a witness, or any person for that matter, can make you a better advocate since you will have a greater grasp of the truth.

Mayor W. Wilson Goode of Philadelphia was in deep trouble over his administration's devastation on May 13, 1985, of a city block housing the radical group MOVE. He insisted that his subordinates misled, misinformed, and disobeyed him. To the panel investigating his responsibility for this destruction of a whole neighborhood, Mayor Goode pleaded that "[K]nowing what I know now, I certainly would be a hands-on kind of person." Then he said, *"I certainly would pose more specific types of questions."*

Questions can be sculpted to elicit a predetermined response, which in turn can be used for propaganda. It is important, therefore, to examine the texture and slant of the question. One example recently is Citizens for Tax Justice, a labor group that seeks to deny tax breaks for business. In April, 1986, the group with fanfare held a news conference to announce the results of its latest poll. Eighty-six percent of the respondents agreed with its position. A typical question was: "Do you agree or disagree that large corporations should start paying their fair share of taxes before there are any increases in any taxes that ordinary and middle-income Americans pay?" Looking at the question, the result is not surprising.

This book, because of shortness of life, will focus on cross-examination in the context of the trial in the courtroom, the crucible of persuasion and verdict. The reason for this approach is that only the trial advocate spends a lifetime learning how to form a prudent question.

There has been a steady deterioration in the quality of

court advocacy in the United States. Trial advocates today do not compare favorably with advocates of the first fifty years of this century. Existing court records show this to be true. What qualities distinguish one trial advocate from another? There are many degrees of excellence, but one essential quality is the mastering of the art of cross-examination. All successful trial advocates, of whatever region, have been accomplished cross-examiners of witnesses.

Of course every trial advocate is unique in his or her own right. The personalities, methods, and styles of trial advocates vary as much as thumbprints. A trial lawyer is doomed to failure if he or she attempts to imitate another trial lawyer, because the essence of successful persuasion is being completely yourself.

A study of the trial advocacy of first-rate American trial lawyers would likely result in a list of ten qualities of excellence: a thorough understanding of human nature; clear, logical thinking and presentation; communicating in direct, simple, coherent thoughts; judgment or a sense of proportion in evaluating and reacting to everything that occurs during the trial; self-discipline; conveying the impression of authority; a dignified and courteous manner; a personality allowing the advocate to assert influence on everyone with whom he comes in contact; compulsiveness for thorough preparation; and the absence of trickery and subterfuge.

Some accomplished trial advocates have an extraordinary capacity for quick thinking and quick decisions, others do not. Some accomplished trial advocates have an extraordinary knowledge of the applicable statutes and court decisions, others do not. Emory R. Buckner, dean of the American bar more than fifty years ago, summarized what trial advocacy is all about in two addresses: "The Trial of Cases," delivered before the Association of the Bar of the City of New York, and "The Lawyer in Court," delivered before the Chicago Bar Association. Buckner emphasized that preparation (or getting all the relevant facts before the start of the contest) was the trial's single most important event. He stressed the importance of the advocate's exercising judgment, or a sense of proportion, in evaluating and reacting to each occurrence at the trial, the importance of learning the law applicable to the case, and the trial lawyer's ethical obligations, which preclude the use of fraudulent devices and forbid the use or tolerance of false testimony during the trial. Most of all Buckner stressed the importance and difficulty of cross-examining the adversary's witnesses.

Buckner was a master of the art of cross-examination. The fact that he was an eminent trial advocate and a master of cross-examination is not a coincidence. They go together. A trial advocate must master the art of cross-examination to be accomplished at his profession. A study of the trials of such great trial lawyers as Patrick Henry, Daniel Webster, Abraham Lincoln, Joseph H. Choate, John Marshall Harlan, J. Edward Lumbard, and John W. Davis reveals that they were masters of the art of cross-examination.

Many of us have heard of Patrick Henry's cross-examination of the chief witness in the abortion-murder trial of Richard Randolph and his sister-in-law Nancy Randolph. The direct testimony of the witness (a daughter of

Henry's old political enemy Archibald Cary) was totally discredited on cross-examination by Patrick Henry, with Henry's cocounsel, the future chief justice of the United States Supreme Court, John Marshall, sitting at Henry's side. This witness had testified on direct that while peeking through a keyhole into Nancy Randolph's bedroom, she saw Nancy Randolph undressing and determined that she was pregnant—the sole testimony on this crucial fact. Henry, relying upon the extensive preparation of his cocounsel, skillfully developed during cross-examination that the chief witness was a "nosybody" who was always peeking through keyholes and eavesdropping on other people's conversations. Henry continually appealed to her vanity and enticed her to convey to the jury exactly what kind of person she really was. Henry was so skillful that he convinced her to get down on the floor on her knees and demonstrate for the jury which eye she used to peek through the keyhole. The jury broke out in laughter and at the same time became convinced that she was not a satisfactory witness to rely upon in a murder trial. Henry's client was acquitted.

Recall Abraham Lincoln's cross-examination of the alleged eyewitness to the murder of James Metzker in the trial of Duff Armstrong. The trial was a subject of a Pulitzer Prize–winning play, *Abe Lincoln in Illinois,* and also a movie starring Henry Fonda as Lincoln. By extensive preparation, Lincoln, acting with the precision of a surgeon, refuted the credibility of the alleged eyewitness to the murder by establishing on cross-examination that this witness could not have seen the fight that allegedly resulted in the murder because the fight occurred at night when there was no moonlight. Lincoln further established that the alleged murder weapon produced by the prosecutor was not the weapon that his client allegedly had in his possession. Lincoln furthermore established through medical testimony that the deceased could have died of accidental causes. Lincoln's client was acquitted.

Some of us have also heard of Emory Buckner's cross-examination of Senator Guy D. Goff in the trial of former United States Attorney General Harry Daugherty (during the Harding administration), in which Buckner effectively destroyed the credibility of Senator Goff. By extensive preparation, Buckner artfully intertwined Goff's present testimony with his prior grand jury testimony and ultimately pushed Goff into a corner where he had to either admit the ultimate facts pursued by Buckner or admit to personal wrongdoing. Goff admitted the facts that resulted in Daugherty's codefendant being convicted. The jury could not reach a verdict as to Daugherty's guilt or innocence after two days of deliberations. The first vote of the jury had been eleven to one for a conviction, and there it stood for two days. For some time thereafter there were discussions at the United States attorney's office about the one holdout on the jury, but foul play could never be established.

The Federal Bar Council, an independent group of lawyers practicing before the federal courts and agencies, celebrates each year the memory of Emory R. Buckner with a luncheon attended by members of the bench and bar at which the council's gold medal is given to a person possessing the Buckner qualities of excellence and skill.

Recipients have included Leonard Page Moore, Sylvester J. Ryan, Whitney North Seymour, Sr., Thomas E. Dewey, Orison S. Marden, Charles D. Breitel, Harold R. Tyler, Jr., and Leon Silverman.

* * *

Three journalists in 1984 decided to write a biographical counter-book to Edward I. Koch's *Mayor.* These city hall reporters had to know precisely to what extent they could, in writing a critical review of Koch, count on any cooperation of the mayor himself in providing data or allowing associates and family to do so. On September 11, 1984, they sought an interview with New York City's controversial and colorful chief magistrate. They had only a few minutes of his honor's time, and they had to ask the right questions to get the right answers.

Q. How much cooperation can we expect of you, Mr. Mayor?
KOCH: None.
Q. What should we do if we get allegations about you? Do you want us to come to you so you can respond?
KOCH: I will not aid or assist you in any way.

Would he let his aides and family talk to them? "My family will not talk to you." The future authors of *I, Koch* (Dodd, Mead, 1985) finally asked whether they could have access to the city library containing his interviews, speeches, videos, etc. "Not to write your book," the mayor replied. Wasn't this an arbitrary distinction? they asked. Koch replied, in effect, "I'm the mayor." In the writing of their threatening book the authors knew exactly where they stood in a few minutes of exchange of questions and answers. No blather. Succinct.

* * *

Sometimes a perfectly normal question is needed to elicit the truth. A friend told a social psychologist recently that at a panel seminar there was an endless debate among the panel and the audience about the possible physical and chemical interventions in treating a chronically depressed man. "No one," the friend said, "had thought to ask the man what he was depressed *about.*"

At the start of World War II the story went around that the United States Army spent millions of dollars researching which soldiers should be sent to the warm climates of the South Pacific and which should be sent to the cold northern climates of Europe. After going over budget army officials finally came to the conclusion that the best test for this critical determination was simply to ask the soldiers this question: "Do you like warm weather or cold weather?" The problem was solved.

In the winter of 1913 the New York Armory had a show of modern art featuring the master colorist, artist Henri Matisse. Hardly had the exhibit opened when conservative critics attacked his paintings, drawings, and sculpture with a singular viciousness. A major newspaper editorialized, "We may as well say in the first place that his pictures are ugly, that they are coarse, that they are narrow, that to us they are revolting in their inhumanity." When the Matisse works moved on to the Art

Institute of Chicago, the art students held a protest meeting and burned, in effigy, Matisse's painting *Nu blue.*

The New York Times Magazine published an interview of Matisse at his home in France by journalist Clara T. MacChesney. It was Miss MacChesney's responsibility to ask prudent questions of this maligned artist, who understood little if any English, about what in the world he was up to. She gamely traveled by rail and foot on a blistering hot day, conjuring in her mind what questions she would ask of this artist who had seemingly turned visual arts upside down. Her questions showed her unfamiliarity with art generally and her lack of understanding of Matisse's work. You will note that while the questions were obtuse, Matisse, formerly a law clerk before going into art, gave a somewhat triumphal defense to an apparently hostile American public.

In his studio at Issy-les-Moulineaux, a suburb of Paris, Miss MacChesney started her questions with two dogs lying at their feet and batting flies that buzzed around them. In the current bias of the times ("But *can* Matisse draw?"), she asked him whether he had had any art training.

MATISSE: I began at the École des Beaux-Arts. When I opened my studio, years after, for some time I painted just like anyone else. But things didn't go at all, and I was very unhappy. Then little by little I began to paint as I felt. . . .

MacCHESNEY: [*perplexed*] Do you recognize harmony of color?

MATISSE: [*somewhat ruffled*] I certainly do think of harmony of color, and of composition too. Drawing is for me the art of being able to express myself with line. When an artist or student draws a nude figure with painstaking care, the result is drawing and not emotion. A true artist cannot see color which is not harmonious. . . . He should not copy the walls, or objects on a table, but he should, above all, express a vision of color, the harmony of which corresponds to his feelings. And, above all, one must be honest to oneself.

MacCHESNEY: [*persisting*] But just what is your theory on art?

MATISSE: Well, take the table for example. [*pointing to one nearby on which stood a jar of nasturtiums*] I do not literally paint that table, but the emotion it produces upon me.

MacCHESNEY: But if one hasn't always emotion, what then?

MATISSE: Do not paint. [*pause*] When I came in here to work this morning I had no emotion so I took a horseback ride. When I returned I felt like painting, and I had all the emotion I wanted.

MacCHESNEY: [*nervously*] Tell me, [*pointing to a lumpy clay study of a nude woman with limbs of great length*] why . . . ?

MATISSE: [*holding in his hand the small Javanese statue with head out of proportion to the body*] Is not that beautiful?

MacCHESNEY: [*boldly*] No. I see no beauty where there is lack of proportion. To my mind no sculpture has ever equaled that of the Greeks unless it is a Michael Angelo's [*sic*].

MATISSE: But there you are, back to the classic, the formal. [*voice rising*] We of today are trying to express ourselves today—now—the twentieth century—and not to copy what the Greeks saw and felt in art over two thousand years ago. . . .

MacCHESNEY: [*glancing at the little figure of a dwarf from Java, failing to see anything of beauty and shaking her head*]

MATISSE: Above all, [*swatting a fly*] the great thing is to express one's self.

MacCHESNEY: [*changing the subject*] You painted a canvas of blue tomatoes. Why blue?

MATISSE: Because I see them that way, and I cannot help it if no one else does.

At the closing of this abortive interview, Matisse looked at Clara MacChesney and said softly, 'Oh, do tell the American people that I am a normal man; that I am a devoted husband and father; that I have three fine children; that I go to the theatre, ride a horse, have a big, comfortable home, a fine garden; that I love flowers, et cetera, just like any man."

On leaving she mused that she was positive that she should not "dare when weary, to sit for long in front of his *Cathedrals at Rouen,* confusing in her mind Matisse and Monet. She had, however, the prescience to write in her published interview of Matisse a final sentence of reservation of opinion, "The testimony of time, of the works, will outweight our present speculations."*

* Extracts from Clara T. MacChesney, "A Talk With Matisse, Leader of Post-Impressionists," *The New York Times Magazine,* March 9, 1913.

Leonard Michael tells a story about a lecture he went to by the German sociologist Jürgen Haberman. Afterward a young woman in the lecture hall raised her hand and said, "I'd like to ask a question, but I'm not into words."

* * *

Whether as a court lawyer cross-examining or a layman questioning another person, the care and attention in forming the question and a little preparation of the subject matter can make a significant difference in the nature of the answer received and the result obtained. That important difference is what this book is about. Get into preparation and get into words.

FOREWORD

by Judge Arnold Guy Fraiman

Peter Megargee Brown's observations about the neglected art of questioning and his thirty maxims for mastering the deceptively simple but highly difficult art of cross-examination should be required reading for all trial advocates.

Most of these pragmatisms are based upon his own thirty-six years' experience as a litigator and his observations of such legendary giants of the courtroom as John Marshall Harlan, J. Edward Lumbard, John W. Davis, Lloyd Paul Stryker, Theodore Kiendl, and Whitney North Seymour, Sr. Others are based upon anecdotes concerning earlier experts in the field such as Francis L. Wellman, Joseph H. Choate, Learned Hand, and Max Steuer.

Stated in its barest terms, Mr. Brown's thesis is that if the witness hasn't hurt you, don't cross-examine. If you do cross-examine, have a specific objective in mind, prepare thoroughly to achieve your objective, and once you have accomplished it, sit down. These tenets, which are basically common sense, would not appear to be insuperable, yet I am continually amazed at how often they are ignored or disregarded by experienced trial lawyers.

As a trial judge sitting in New York County for the past sixteen years, I have observed a veritable panoply of litigators in action, ranging from individual practitioners to senior partners in the most prestigious Wall Street law firms. Hardly a trial goes by when there does not occur one of the pitfalls which Mr. Brown warns about in telling fashion: for example, learned counsel on cross-examination will have the witness reiterate all or a substantial part of what he has said on direct, thus emphasizing to the jury what his opponent has tried to establish by calling the witness initially.

It is my custom during trial to make copious notes of what I consider to be key testimony—that is, testimony having a direct bearing on the ultimate factual issues which must be resolved. I keep these notes in thick, hard-covered, ruled ledgers, and over the years I have filled almost twenty of them. As Mr. Brown notes, cross-examination is the most important weapon in a trial lawyer's arsenal for eliciting the truth and for casting doubt on the witness's false testimony. Yet, in leafing through these ledgers recently, one fact stands out: my notes on cross-examination testimony comprise only a small part of each ledger. In other words, in a majority of cases relatively little testimony was elicited on cross-examination that I believed as having any effect on the resolution of essential issues. The reason for this has been apparent to me over the years: basically, many trial counsel have simply not mastered the precepts of cross-examination which are the focus of this little book.

Mr. Brown's thirty dos and don'ts are interestingly illustrated by anecdotes in and out of the courtroom related in a refreshingly breezy style. This compendium is recommended for all courtroom denizens, whether novices or experienced hands.

ARNOLD GUY FRAIMAN,
Retired Justice of the Supreme Court
of the State of New York,
First Judicial District (New York City)

ACKNOWLEDGMENTS

This book would not have been possible without the good-humored encouragement of my wife, Alexandra Stoddard, who proposed publication, and the indefatigable Ann Lauria, administrator at Brown & Seymour, who suffered through the drafts and the anecdotes. I also acknowledge indebtedness to my friends and colleagues Whitney North Seymour, Jr., Claude P. Bordwine, Arthur V. Medel, George E. Diethelm, and Howard W. Burns, as well as Alexandra Brandon Stoddard, Brooke Goodwin Stoddard, and Blair Tillyer Brown Hoyt. Additionally, I record my gratitude to those trial lawyers and cross-examiners who taught so tirelessly the little we have learned: J. Edward Lumbard, John Marshall Harlan, Francis A. Wellman, Theodore Kiendl, Benjamin A. Matthews, and Jacquelin A. Swords.

THE ART OF QUESTIONING

The Art of Questioning: Thirty Maxims of Cross-Examination

One day when he was on a visit to New York City, I had a discussion with Lord Kenneth Diplock, a lord of appeal in ordinary in the British House of Lords, a position which is similar to that of a United States Supreme Court justice. Lord Diplock commented that our American courts are too riddled by technicalities. I agreed. Then he said, "Never mind the technicalities. Justice is a matter of gut feeling."

When, how, and in what manner cross-examination is carried on should be a matter of gut feeling—but only after the most meticulous preparation.

Lord Diplock's associate, Sir Wilfred Bourne, a permanent secretary to the lord chancellor, piped up, "We visited federal court in the Eastern District this morning. It was a narcotics case. An undercover agent had testified regarding his sale to the defendant. The counsel for defendant commenced an aimless cross-examination of the prosecution's main witness, which simply underscored to judge and jury the utter guilt of the defendant beyond a reasonable doubt. What the young defense counsel should have done, I think, was to rise from his chair after direct examination, look the jury in the eye, and say confidently, 'No questions'!"

If you travel around to the various courts you will find that the restraint Sir Wilfred recommended is all too rare. There is a glorious obsession that every witness produced by the adversary must be cross-examined ad nauseam. Aimlessly. Endlessly. Cross-examination is frequently called an art, and in many respects it is. As in other fields of art some have unusual talents for their work, but talented or not, a great deal of hard work is necessary for success. There is no reason why a good lawyer, who is willing to work very hard at it and to acquire the necessary experience in court, cannot become reasonably proficient in cross-examination. Many books have been written and lectures given on the subject, but no writing or lecture can tell you what question to ask, how it should be phrased, when it should be put, or most important, when it should *not* be put. This book is an attempt to clarify the pitfalls that the lawyer and the non-lawyer faces when he takes the floor against a witness or adversary and to help him to be prepared to think on his feet.

Professor John Henry Wigmore in his famous treatise on evidence may have been exaggerating when he proclaimed that cross-examination is "beyond any doubt the greatest legal engine ever invented for the discovery of truth." Nevertheless, and whether or not cross-examination is an art, it necessitates: (1) the utmost ingenuity on our part; (2) habits of logical thought; (3) instant retrieval; (4) clearness of perception; (5) infinite patience; (6) ice-cold self-control; (7) the power to read a witness's mind; (8) the ability to judge character and weakness by face, sound, behavior, and smell; (9) talent enough to appreciate a witness's motive, however piously camouflaged; (10) the skill to act with force; (11) penetrating knowledge of the subject matter; (12) an extreme sense of caution; and (13) the instinct to uncover surgically the witness's weak point, the elusive jugular vein. Extreme caution and finding the jugular are the principal requirements of a competent cross-examination.

Why is it, I wonder, that the earlier books on cross-examination have a richer conveyance of reality than the crop of current materials? One answer may be that in the old days the teaching came from barristers who had thirty or forty years of battle experience in the courtroom. In those days there was little time spent on discovery and luxury motions. The veteran trial lawyer went from trial to trial and was often unemployed while awaiting his next case. It was during the periods of unemployment that barristers wrote down their hard-earned principles of advocacy, including one of the most important (and today neglected) aspects, cross-examination.

The early masters understood better than today's professors the importance of *foregoing* cross-examination and the stupidity of having an adverse witness repeat and thus reinforce all that was said so damagingly on direct. They were aware of the utter destruction of a client's case by introduction of bad taste, constant sarcasm, showing off, wise-guy exchanges, and unfair tactics. Early commentators also recognized the deadly pitfalls of displaying before jury and judge crude manners, mean conduct, and insulting behavior toward the witness or his counsel.

Expert barristers knew that such abuses tend to result in an adverse verdict because of one cardinal rule: juries sympathize with witnesses. The cross-examiner, the jury knows, has been specially trained and has the advantage of having studied the entire case. The witness is at a disadvantage because he or she is being subjected to the lawyer's sometimes tricky, hostile, or technical questions.

Most trial lawyers perform with less skill and result during cross-examination than during other portions of the trial process. One reason may be that they make the mistake of not preparing a comprehensive cross-examination witness sheet before trial, an outline of what the lawyer hopes to accomplish with a particular witness based on everything he has learned prior to examination. Even though he has labored over a cross-examination sheet, the expert trial lawyer may still decide at the time not to cross-examine at all, to skip some of the areas of inquiry, or to improvise. But to have no cross-examination witness sheet knitted to the theory of a case is flying by your britches in an uncharted sky.

The constant references to cross-examination as an art form have induced lawyers to believe that cross-examination is intuitive and that without careful preparation they can rise to the occasion and mesmerize the witness, jury, and court. Despite some cute barristers' anecdotes, spirited bestselling paperbacks, and nightly television programs, it isn't necessarily so. More cross-examinations are suicidal than homicidal. When in doubt, don't ask a question. When in doubt, don't cross-examine. Do only what's necessary, and then get the hell out.

Here are thirty maxims of cross-examination distilled from personal experience, reading records, and hearing stories from trial veterans. I hope, without paralysis by analysis, they will help future inquisitors avoid at least a few of the pitfalls that lie in waiting for unwary neophytes. I've fallen into the pitfalls many times in thirty-six years.

MAXIM I

There Is No Substitute for Preparation

John Marshall Harlan was trained as a cross-examiner by Emory R. Buckner (1877–1941), one of America's foremost trial lawyers and a top cross-examiner. While on the Supreme Court, Justice Harlan reminisced about his former chief in New York: "The New York Bar has given to the country many distinguished lawyers, but few of them, I venture to say, have left so deep an imprint on the next generation of the profession as has Emory R. Buckner . . . His influence was not of the pedantic sort, but was born of the human and professional stuff that sticks with those who were exposed to it." Justice Harlan served under Emory Buckner when Buckner was United States attorney in the Southern District of New York. It was Harlan's habit to commence preparing cross-examination of major witnesses as soon as the case was assigned to him. He never waited until the judge said, "You may cross-examine."

Harlan developed the cross-examination witness sheet to perfection. He never rose to cross-examine without having carefully prepared a witness sheet setting forth what he hoped to accomplish, together with the factual building blocks necessary to reach that goal. In every case those building blocks were specifically cited to transcript, deposition, and document exhibit. Harlan learned this discipline from Buckner and meticulously passed on the procedure to those who later assisted him on the trial of civil and criminal cases.

Every able cross-examiner I can think of was trained by someone. There is in the courtroom a genealogy of acquired skills. Such talents do not come out of the blue. Harlan not only carefully prepared in advance but exercised extreme caution at all times. He was a true bomb-squader.

An example of Harlan's expertise in cross-examination was his conduct in the early 1950s during the New York State Crime Commission public hearings, ferreting out the relationship between organized crime and government. The Staten Island hearings commenced at the courthouse in West Brighton before the crime commission with Joseph M. Proskauer as chairman. Harlan, as chief counsel, conducted his cross-examination at counsels' table flanked by First Assistant Leslie H. Arps, myself, and Julio Nunez as so-called bird dogs, aka assistant counsel.

Our undercover investigation had revealed elements of corruption in the district attorney's office and relationships between organized crime (the Dallessios), Democratic District Attorney Herman Methfessel, and Republican County Leader Edward A. Ruppell, who was then on the Democratic payroll as commissioner of public works. District Attorney Methfessel was a major subject of the inquiry. Harlan's brilliant cross-examination of

County Leader Ruppell revealed a network of local political chicanery.

The public hearings caused quite a stir in the newspapers and on television. During Harlan's cross-examination, Governor Thomas E. Dewey felt compelled to supercede Methfessel as district attorney and designate a special prosecutor, William B. Herland. (Later, Herland became a federal judge.)

The day after his appointment Herland came to court to follow Harlan's cross-examination of Ruppell. In the course of the examination Herland tapped me on the shoulder and asked me to suggest that Mr. Harlan ask Ruppell a certain question. Herland wrote down the question and handed it to me. I passed it to Arps, who looked at the note somewhat critically. Arps put the note on the far right corner of the counsel table within the view of Harlan, who was engaged in vigorous close-up cross-examination of Ruppell. At a pause Harlan picked up the note, glanced at it, and whispered to Arps. Arps turned to me and whispered, "He said, 'Does Herland know the answer to the question?' " I turned to Herland and asked him, "Do you know the answer to your question?" He shook his head. That was the end of that. Harlan never asked a question when he didn't know the answer. President Eisenhower later appointed Harlan to a seat on the Second Circuit Court of Appeals and in 1956 to the United States Supreme Court, where he continued his exceptional craftsmanship, now questioning the best appellate counsel in the nation.

Sergeant Ballantine's *Experiences* illustrates the danger of asking a question in a courtroom context without knowing the answer. During the cross-examination of a witness in a murder trial, a famous barrister was induced by the defendant's solicitor to ask a question without knowing the answer. The barrister did so against his own judgment, and the answer later convicted his client. Upon receiving the answer, the barrister turned to the solicitor and said through clenched teeth, *"Go home; cut your throat; and when you meet your client in hell, beg his pardon."*

MAXIM II

Watch Out for the Judge

Joseph M. Proskauer, the peripatetic chairman of the New York State Crime Commission, had a busy and successful career first as a trial lawyer and then as an occasionally exasperated New York Supreme Court judge. When he realized that as a matter of temperament he could not stand to watch lesser minds fumble with witnesses in his courtroom, he resigned from the bench and went back to private practice. His cross-examination from the bench in the course of the crime commission's public hearings exhibited a knack for nailing recalcitrant witnesses.

The impact of a judge's intervention to ask a devastating question during live examination can be so severe as to determine the outcome of a trial. In many cases you will desire rather than resist pointed questions from the judge on your cross-examination. An "impartial" judge may provide you with a bonanza question and answer to reiterate to the jury on summation. From the vantage of the bench the judge can fling a bull's eye question that leaves one party's case impaled. So watch out for the judge.

In the *BusStop Shelter* case in the Southern District of New York, the prosecutor sought to show defendant Jack Bronston's double-dealing as practicing lawyer and public officer in bidding for the New York City franchise. Defense lawyer Louis Nizer argued that Bronston was an honest man whose only interest was seeing that the best company be given the franchise. The prosecution called Bronston's estranged partner Howard Schneider to the stand to show the conflict at their law firm, where another bidder client was represented.

On cross-examination Nizer skillfully brought out that Bronston had never approached partner Schneider for information or background about *BusStop,* the firm's bidder, and that Bronston had made clear his opinion that competitive bidding for the franchise was best for all concerned. "Competitive bidding," Nizer had emphasized in his opening, "is what the case is about, not 'double-dealing'."

Just as witness Schneider's testimony was being concluded, Judge Milton Pollack cast a bolt of lightning with a question of his own: "Was Mr. Bronston free to promote the mutually exclusive interests of a competitor?"

Nizer and Bronston were thunderstruck. Bronston's face became beet red. Nizer rose to object. Schneider answered, "No." Court observers believed that the judge's annihilating question and Schneider's flat answer became the crux of the case.

* * *

In a recent case in Queens, New York, involving construction of a bitterly contested will, one of the main issues was the adequacy of the will being offered for probate. The will had been awkwardly (but unintentionally) drawn to permit inheritance by beneficiaries in the event of a "common disaster," but would allow intestacy to apply otherwise. There was no "common disaster" so the will was without effect. Both the husband and wife had died. The lawyer who prepared the joint will executed by husband and wife Sam and Dorothy R. was on the witness stand being questioned when the judge suddenly interjected:

THE COURT: [*angrily*] Did you know who her blood kin were?

THE WITNESS: I never—

THE COURT: You don't even take a family tree? You didn't take any information about who their next of kin were? How do you draw a will without knowing who the next of kin are?

THE WITNESS: [*defensively*] As far as they [husband and wife wanting a will] were concerned, they didn't have any children, and their next of kin to each other were themselves.

THE COURT: [*zinger*] Are children the only next of kin?

THE WITNESS: Now, listen, I'm trying to explain to you, Your Honor. If you want to lecture me, I'll be happy to listen to you. I took what history I could from both of them, and I got to the substance of what they wanted. What he wanted was what she had because everything was in her name. She wanted what he had, if he had anything. Each expected to outlive the other, and then they were advised that they should get a new will and, whoever they wanted to leave their assets to, they could. I gave the correct advice. If you don't feel it was correct advice, I can't help that.

THE COURT: I wasn't there.

THE WITNESS: You weren't there, and I wasn't there—

THE COURT: [*staring at the lawyer's witness*] What did you just say?

THE WITNESS: "You weren't there, and I wasn't there." I was there. I'm sorry.

THE COURT: That's what I thought you said.

THE WITNESS: Sometimes you get caught up in your own emotions. If that's what you want, that's what you get.

THE COURT: That's not what I want. I'm not here to confuse you.

THE WITNESS: Your Honor, your questioning me on this will, I think it's a perfectly good will. I have drawn up many of them, and you have passed many of them before.

THE COURT: Do me a favor. When you go back to your office, do me a personal favor and *look at every will you have in the file and then make sure that those wills don't come before this court again.*

THE WITNESS: Your Honor, you have been passing them right along.

THE COURT: I have been passing these wills?

THE WITNESS: You have passed these wills by before. I have had other cases here where I have probated the exact same will.

THE COURT: You had a survivor?

THE WITNESS: We have a survivor here.

THE COURT: No, you don't, sir. If Mrs. R. were before the court because Sam had assets in his name, Sam's will would be before the court.

THE WITNESS: Then it would be a good will. Then it would be a good will, right?

THE COURT: Yes, sir.

THE WITNESS: Okay. Unfortunately, before I advised her to make up a new will—now, before she had made up a new will, she died. I advised her to make up a new will. The will that would have been before this court if we probated it when Sam died would have been a good will that you would have passed on. This is what you said.

THE COURT: But if she died ten minutes after Sam, it's not a good will.

THE WITNESS: [*weakly*] Then it would have been an intestacy.

THE COURT: And that's what she wanted?

THE WITNESS: I don't know what she wanted. I told her—

THE COURT: What would be the purpose of going to a lawyer? Why pay a fee?

THE WITNESS: She didn't come to me to draw up a second will. I wanted her to come to me.

THE COURT: No, the first will.

THE WITNESS: The first will covered their situation. It covered their situation.

THE COURT: As you recall it?

THE WITNESS: As I feel it did. With thirty-five years of practice, that's what I felt. I know I'm not a specialist in this field of law—

JUDGE: Well, the record is there. I must admit to you that I have about forty-five hundred wills filed in this county per year. I have been surrogate thirteen years. This phraseology, this will, comes out of a form book where the author of that book was advised to take it out.

WITNESS: Well, I didn't know about that.

JUDGE: But because of the matter of personal pride, he never did. That's not the best language.

WITNESS: I would say you are right in the sense that I'm getting to be an antique, and I should retire.

JUDGE: [*angrily*] I have no idea *what* you plan to do with your life.

The judge then ordered the will-drafting lawyer to return to the estate all fees he had received for the administration of the estate.

* * *

A garrulous and somewhat flamboyant defense counsel, Nick Atlas, wanted to introduce a photograph in a jury trial before Judge Edward Weinfeld. Atlas stepped to the bench and for twenty minutes recited why the photograph should be admitted under the rules of evidence. Finally Atlas concluded, "Your Honor, a picture is worth a thousand words." The judge looked down at Atlas and said, "You have had *both*. We will now receive the photograph."

MAXIM III

Focus Your Fire on the Main Adverse Witness

One of the major exciting American trials of this century is *United States* v. *Alger Hiss.* Hiss, a brilliant lawyer, darling of the New Deal, a top Department of State public servant, advisor to President Roosevelt at Yalta, was charged with perjury in the course of grand jury hearings in federal court in New York. Congressman Richard M. Nixon was convinced Hiss was a spy for the Soviet Union, but the statute of limitations on espionage had run its course. The ebullient and mustachioed Assistant United States Attorney Thomas F. Murphy was chosen as the prosecutor. (Subsequently, Mr. Murphy became police commissioner of the city of New York and currently is a United States district court judge.)

The celebrated Alger Hiss case still lives on after three decades, the emotional reverberations echoing down to the present day. Early in 1986 Richard Nixon wrote to *The New York Times* that there are lessons to be learned from the Hiss case. In doing so, Mr. Nixon added more fuel to the fire: Chambers, he said, seventy times collected espionage documents from Hiss and had delivered them to a Soviet contact; reporters were obsessed with style, thought Chambers "poorly dressed, pudgy, undistinguished in appearance and in background," while they saw Hiss as the epitome of the fashionable

Eastern establishment with impeccable social and intellectual qualifications. Nixon suggested that with Adlai Stevenson and John Foster Dulles as Hiss's character witnesses, Hiss, in effect, pleaded "innocence by association." Mr. Nixon then recalled the most moving part of the earlier Hiss hearing in Washington, near the end of Chambers's accusation testimony, when Congressman Nixon had asked Chambers this question: "Can you search your memory now to see what motive you can have for accusing Mr. Hiss of being a communist? . . . Is there any grudge you have against Mr. Hiss over anything he has done to you?" Chambers answered:

> The story has spread that in testifying against Mr. Hiss I am working out some old grudge or motives of revenge or hatred. I do not hate Mr. Hiss. We were close friends, but we are caught in a tragedy of history. Mr. Hiss represents the concealed enemy against which we are all fighting and I am fighting. I have testified against him with remorse and pity, but in a moment of history in which this nation now stands, so help me God, I cannot do otherwise.

The day after Mr. Nixon's broadside against Hiss, (*The New York Times,* Op-Ed, January 8, 1986), Alger Hiss responded with eloquence and force, again denying the charges against him made thirty-seven years ago. He said his case was tried in the hysteria of the early cold war year of 1949, after the sensational hearings by the House Committee on Un-American Activities. Hiss concluded, "Once more, I assert that I did not engage in espionage. It is still simply Whittaker Chambers's word against mine. In calmer times my word has been accepted, and it will be again. My case seems to be a barometer of the cold war."

Journalist and former communist Whittaker Chambers was the principal if not the sole witness against Hiss. Chambers's testimony would be devastating if found credible by the jury. Consequently, Alger Hiss's defense counsel brought in suave psychiatrist Dr. Carl Binger as an expert witness to destroy Chambers as a "psychopathic liar." The upshot of the direct examination of Dr. Binger was that Whittaker Chambers had an evil, sordid background of making false accusations.

But then prosecutor Thomas F. Murphy rose to his full height of six feet seven inches to cross-examine Dr. Binger. He turned the case around. Hiss was convicted. Murphy told me that he had spent more than one hundred hours in preparation for his cross-examination of Dr. Binger.

To appreciate the art of Murphy's questioning of Hiss, it must be kept in mind that the main point of Murphy's cross-examination was not only to attack Binger's expert testimony. He determined to show that Dr. Binger's *conclusion* was erroneous, not because Binger himself was not qualified as an expert, but because the *facts* which Binger had were inadequate for his conclusion. This was a brilliant decision, though perhaps a subtle one to those not familiar with courtroom strategies. If Murphy had attacked Binger's expertise, he would have been forced to deal in the fields of psychology and psychiatry, areas in which Dr. Binger clearly had the edge. But by simply sticking to the facts, Murphy neutralized Binger's expertise and was able to keep control of his cross-examination, as the following excerpts demonstrate. (Other excerpts from the transcript of this trial appear later in this book to illustrate other maxims.)

PROSECUTOR THOMAS MURPHY: [*laying the foundation for his factual attack*] Now, Doctor, would it help at all to a psychiatrist such as yourself in forming a professional opinion, a professional psychiatric opinion of a person's personality, to have detailed information concerning that person's early childhood? For instance, his or her relationship with parents, the relationship with brothers and sisters, in the early formative years? Is that important, Doctor, when you, as a psychiatrist, are going to form an opinion as to a person's personality?

DR. BINGER: Certainly.

Q. You didn't have any of that in this case, did you, Doctor?

A. Not as much as I would have liked to have had.

Zinger!

* * *

Another sample:

PROSECUTOR MURPHY: [*tight closed-end question controlling the witness*] Doctor, are you able to tell us as a psychiatric expert which part of . . . Mr. Chambers's testimony . . . is true or false? Can you do that, Doctor?

A. Certainly not.

Q. No psychiatrist can, can he?

A. I can't speak for others. I can't.

Q. Talking about other psychiatrists, Doctor, would you say that other psychiatrists, let us say as qualified as yourself, might perhaps have a different opinion based upon the facts that you have here?

A. [*smoothly*] I should be very surprised if they did. I have talked to a great many of them.

Q. Well, whether you would be surprised or not, Doctor, what is your answer to the question? Would you say that perhaps another qualified psychiatrist would have a different opinion than you do?

A. Well, it would be, naturally. That is something I don't know about.

Q. [*driving in*] Well, the science of medicine and psychiatry is not quite an exact science, is it, Doctor?

A. Of course not.

Q. And doctors have been known to disagree on diagnoses?

A. Frequently.

Q. And some doctors have been known to be wrong on diagnoses?

A. Frequently.

Q. Have you ever been wrong, Doctor?

A. Certainly.

MAXIM IV

Be a Skillful Surgeon

Lloyd Paul Stryker was a trial lawyer and cross-examiner of flair and penetration. His book, *The Art of Advo-*

cacy, has recently been reissued in paperback by the Charles Evans Hughes Press of the New York State Bar Foundation. When at Yale Law School my class invited him to come to speak to us. I went to his room to pick him up before his lecture and found him dressing in front of a mirror while rehearsing the peroration of his speech. He revealed that English barristers invariably rehearse their examinations and speeches, while Americans, believing such preparation unnecessary, vain, or even shameful, are reluctant to do so. So English speakers are invited for after-dinner flourishes more frequently than Americans are. A lesson here.

Stryker had virtually a one-man law office. He characterized himself as a barrister who would try the tough cases and not steal other lawyers' clients. He was highly successful, particularly as defense counsel, and was retained by Alger Hiss in his first trial for perjury, which resulted in a hung jury. Stryker considered that outcome a great disappointment, but looking back now, he did very well in what might be deemed the dawn of the McCarthy era.

Even as he aged, Stryker had a youthful, vigorous exuberance. He loved the courtroom and delighted in being its centerpiece. He relished the opening, lacing it with literary allusions. He savored the cross-examinations and his rehearsed summation. I suspect that cross-examination was his favorite part of the trial, for he viewed it as his laboratory for the study of man. Like a surgeon, he dissected the character and motives of witnesses. He had the knack of distinguishing between truth and falsity, sincerity and sham, the genuine and the spurious.

His favorite remark was that a good cross-examiner is a product of a generation of witnesses. He said that a cross-examiner's education

> never ends, and each witness called affords him a new study. Each one presents the problem: has he told the whole truth or only part of it? Has he tried to give his honest recollection, or is it only the fallibility of memory that has interfered? Is he testifying from some bias that even he does not appreciate? Is there something he has omitted that would be helpful to your client? And finally, is he an out-and-out perjurer, a bold intentional liar under oath?

Stryker believed that the answers to these questions would determine the nature of his cross-examination. On the correctness of his judgment hung his client's fate.

Stryker was a keen observer. He would watch carefully how the witness behaved in the courtroom and on the stand. He would rivet his eyes on the quarry during direct examination. He did not, as most of us do, sit there, eyes down, making notes. He studied the specific mannerisms of the witness. He looked for clues in the ways the individual expressed herself or himself. He listened for the variations in tone of voice caused by the tightening of vocal cords. He noticed pauses. He noted flashes of anxiety, dryness of mouth, moistening of lips, hesitations, discomfort, and uncalled-for repetitions of coached material. He watched for stammer and for needless reference by the witness to counsel's name: "I never went there, Mr. Prosecutor." Eyes were of particular interest. How and when did pupils shift and dart? When did eyes narrow or blink? The giveaway laugh and wipe of forehead. Hands wring, cling, scratch, and readjust.

Legs shuffle. A hand touches the pocket with notes taken from his lawyers on what to avoid at all costs. . . .

To follow Stryker's example, you should be a good surgeon; *observe* your subject, and then go for the jugular.

* * *

During a waterfront investigation by the New York State Crime Commission, the mayor of Jersey City, John V. Kenny (successor to the political spoils of Mayor Hague), was subpoenaed and brought by District Attorney Frank Hogan before the New York County Grand Jury. He was sworn and then directly asked if eleven days earlier he had met in a New York hotel suite with notorious racketeer Anthony (Tony Bender) Strollo to discuss jurisdictional spoils of dock extortion and related rackets rife in the New York–New Jersey waterfront port. Mayor Kenny denied absolutely that he knew or ever had met Strollo. He didn't know why celebrity singer Phil Regan took him that night from Toots Shor's bar at 11:30 P.M. to Regan's suite at the Warwick Hotel for an hour and thirty minutes. Kenny insisted he would not know Strollo "if he walked in this room."

The grand jury testimony of John V. Kenny shows how he lied:

Q. [*by the District Attorney*] Do you know to this date, as you sit there, why [Phil] Regan brought you to that hotel suite?

KENNY: No, I do not, Mr. Prosecutor.

Q. You don't have any idea?

KENNY: No, sir.

Six days later, fearing perhaps that Regan had squealed or the hotel room had been bugged, Mayor Kenny asked to appear again before the grand jury to recant or correct his previous "misstatements." He then admitted meeting and conversing with racketeer Anthony (Tony Bender) Strollo in Regan's suite in connection with Strollo's heavy role on the criminal-infested waterfront. Kenny conceded further that Strollo was successor in the rackets to racket boss Joe Adonis and was now himself in a position to control the underworld elements on the piers. He offered Kenny his aid. Subsequently Mayor Kenny was subpoenaed and testified once before the New York State Crime Commission. After resisting a second subpoena by insistence that he was a responsible public official, Mayor Kenny fled back across the state line to the sanctuary of New Jersey. There, safe in his bailiwick, Kenny called in the press to complain that New York's crime commission investigators were "biased" and out to "get him."

The suggestion of Mayor Kenny that he was merely urging Anthony (Tony Bender) Strollo to keep the waterfront free of criminal elements reminds me of eminent trial lawyer Theodore Kiendl's first day as special counsel of the New York State Crime Commission to inquire into New York waterfront racketeering. The infamous Anthony (Tony) Anatasia had been subpoenaed to appear before the commission and answer Kiendl's questions. Anastasia arrived and sat in the witness chair, cap in hand, eyes dark and brooding. There was silence as Theodore Kiendl entered the room and took his seat at counsel table. He wore a dark blue fitted Saville Row suit, a stiff white collar, and a full head of silver hair. He then said in a sonorous tone, "Mr. Anastasia, my name is Theodore Kiendl. The governor of this state, Thomas E. Dewey, has appointed me as special counsel of the crime commission in order to *clean up the New York–New Jersey waterfront!*"

There was a pause. Tony Anastasia raised his cap and said, "Mr. Kiendl, thanka youa very much for your cooperation."

* * *

Paul Ekman, a professor of psychology at the University of California in San Francisco, suggests that catching liars is an art anyone can learn. People show telltale signs, he says, when they lie. "Liars usually do not monitor, control, and disguise all of their behavior." Body language provides a rich source of information because certain facial and muscle movements cannot be faked.

While not everyone can be expected to spend a great bulk of their time trying to be experts at catching liars, being sensitive and aware of certain signals of lying will be an effective tool in a good questioner's arsenal.

Watch carefully, and be a skillful surgeon.

MAXIM **V**

Take the Liars over the Coals

Although some witnesses tell a fairly accurate story, many more exaggerate, are biased, or their version is somehow "slanted," to use Emily Dickinson's word. The party producing a witness for his side invariably earns from the witness some kind of internal loyalty, shown in the witness's desire to uphold the position of the one who calls him. This is especially true of expert witnesses. This slant of testimony, or doglike loyalty, can sometimes be unconscious on the witness' part, so care must be taken not to attack him directly as if he were a liar and a cheat.

On the other hand, from time to time you will encounter adverse witnesses who are actually lying through their teeth on material points at issue. Such perjurers must be met head on, and every fair and just means must be employed to destroy the witness's credibility. He must be exposed for what he is: a liar.

While in the United States attorney's office I happened to come across what seemed to be a cabal of perjurers. This story of cross-examination has overtones of Damon Runyon, but every bit is true.

Assigned to prosecute Orlando Delli Paoli, a middle-level Mafia chief, for wholesale trafficking in heroin, I had earlier obtained a jury conviction of Orlando Delli Paoli for transportation of illegal alcohol. Now Delli Paoli was faced with another trial as an organization criminal for selling two and a half kilos of heroin. He was afraid, for the evidence was strong against him.

One winter day Delli Paoli appeared in court with his counsel, young dapper Julian A. Frank, and pleaded guilty to the narcotics indictment. The judge was an ascetic bachelor, John W. Clancy. Judge Clancy asked Delli Paoli whether he understood the charges of the indictment, and when he said he did, Judge Clancy accepted his plea of guilty. Two days later the grave judge sentenced Delli Paoli to five years' imprisonment, which together with his alcohol conviction would put him away for a long time.

Five days after sentencing, Delli Paoli through another attorney sought to withdraw his plea of guilty and to vacate sentence, alleging that his lawyer Julian Frank had coerced him into offering a guilty plea. On hearing of Delli Paoli's turnabout, Judge Clancy granted him a hearing to present his claim. For two days Delli Paoli and his fellow witnesses presented what seemed to be perjured testimony. They claimed that Delli Paoli was really innocent but had been forced by his lawyer, Frank, to plead guilty because the law enforcement authorities were out to frame him repeatedly. Underlying their claim was the allegation that Julian Frank, a former assistant U.S. attorney in the previous administration, had represented to Delli Paoli that if he pleaded guilty Frank would "arrange" with myself and Judge Clancy to let him off lightly. The fix was in.

Delli Paoli called four witnesses and testified himself. I called one witness—Julian Frank.

Delli Paoli testified that Frank had told him that he had spoken with Judge Clancy, who was going to be very lenient and give him two or three years at the most. On cross-examination Delli Paoli finally conceded that if he had been sentenced to only one or two years, he would not have brought on the motion to vacate his sentence of five years.

Julian A. Frank, the government's witness, flatly

denied the evidence offered by Delli Paoli and his cohorts.

Judge Clancy, after his own cross-examination and the prosecutor's, stated on the record, his face red and stern, "Of course, they are all lying on their face. . . . There is no substance to their testimony at all. I think having to listen to them imposes such a duty on the judge that it is an outrage."

Then, visibly angry with the deceit around him, he said, "The finding is that there isn't a witness that came in before me that told any truth at all. In fact I doubt the names of some of them."

In this bizarre case every witness had lied.

Downcast, Delli Paoli went off to serve his time. Having crossed his client Delli Paoli, Julian Frank apparently feared for his life. A few months later I received a telephone call from a reporter at *The New York Times.* He said, "I wonder whether you would have any comment on some information that just has come in. An airplane flying from New York to Miami has exploded over North Carolina, killing everyone on board. One of the passengers on that plane was Julian A. Frank, and I have just learned that he had taken out $7 million of life insurance." A bomb device was located next to his seat. Appalled, after a moment I said, "No comment."

MAXIM VI

Develop Your Sixth Sense for Striking Oil

A favorite advocate was John W. Davis. He and his father were jury trial lawyers in West Virginia. Davis knew a great deal about people, life, and literature. He was a presidential candidate in 1924. He subsequently became a trial lawyer at a New York firm where he glowed for years as a leader of the bar. A superb advocate in every way, he had this to say about cross-examination:

> Undoubtedly cross-examination is among the most difficult of the arts of the advocate. It is also one of the most valuable. Every person familiar with the courts has seen cases won almost solely because of its skillful use, and also, sad to say, cases wholly lost by a bungling, an indiscreet, or an overconfident cross-examiner; just where the line lies between a cross-examination that is helpful and one that is harmful only experience can teach. Only experience can give the advocate that sixth sense which tells him when he has reached dangerous ground, when he may advance, when he must retreat, and when he can risk his case upon a single throw.

Davis, who had a mixed bag of cases, in his later days at 15 Broad Street adjacent to Wall Street, liked to say to young lawyers about cross-examination, "When you strike oil [he pronounced it 'ile'] stop boring; many a man has bored clean through and let the oil run out of the bottom."

Once a grande dame complained to him in his office

about the size of his fee for a written opinion involving a large trust. Davis looked up at her, then at his assistant. "Well, madam" he said in his soft Southern accent, "would you prefer that my assistant sign the opinion?"

Framing the right question may be the product of a lifetime and the wall of a library. During the televised McCarthy army hearings before a Senate committee in 1954, Senator McCarthy at one point declared in a smear that the army's counsel, bow-tied, avuncular Joseph Welch, had employed in his law firm and now at his side at counsel table one Fred Fisher, who had been, Senator McCarthy charged dramatically, a member of the legal arm of the Communist party.

Joseph Welch quickly admitted that young Fred Fisher had told him that he had been a member of the left-wing Lawyers' Guild while in law school. That, he said, was some time ago. Senator McCarthy maliciously persisted in attacking Welch's aide, Fisher. Finally Joseph Welch, grim-faced and explosive, shot his own bolt into McCarthy: "Let us not assassinate this lad further, Senator. You have done enough. Have you no sense of decency, sir, at long last? Have you left no sense of decency?"

Note the short two sentences of admonition. Then two stunning questions about decency—just the right rapier to decapitate his adversary. Ah, the eloquence and penetration of the forthright put-down in the heat of controversy. Joseph Welch, an old hand in the courtroom, never bored through to let the oil out; he knew precisely when to stop.

MAXIM **VII**

Exercise Self-Control

Francis L. Wellman in his classic *The Art of Cross-Examination* (first published by Macmillan in 1903) emphasized the need for self-control on the part of the cross-examiner, particularly when he or she had elicited an answer damaging to the client's cause. Damaging answers occur in court more often than cross-examiners like to admit.

If you show by your face or manner when a damaging answer hurts, or if you bolt and retire behind the lectern to go sheepishly on to another subject, you may harm your cause irrevocably. We often see a cross-examiner pulverized by a damaging answer. He gulps, he blushes, and then after allowing the answer its full lethal effect, he may go forward, but not often in control of the witness.

Wellman suggests that a really experienced trial lawyer, rather than showing surprise, will seem to take the answer as a matter of course and let it fall perfectly flat. He will proceed with the next question as if nothing had happened, or give the witness an incredulous smile as if to say, "Who do you suppose would believe that for a minute?" Theodore Kiendl's response to a damaging answer was to emit a doubtful, suspicious "uhm-mm."

During the retrial of Claus von Bülow, Maria Schrallhammer, Mrs. von Bülow's frantically loyal maid, was introduced as the prosecution's strongest witness, as she had been in the first trial. Her testimony centered on finding insulin in von Bülow's black bag, which was the cornerstone of the prosecution's case.

Thomas Puccio, the chief defense lawyer, in his cross-examination sought to discredit her testimony by pointing out various discrepancies, but every time he showed a discrepancy, Miss Schrallhammer was ready with a plausible answer.

Why had she not told Richard Kuh, an ex–district attorney and hired private investigator, about the bottle of insulin, the needle, and the syringe she said she found in the little black bag in Mr. von Bülow's closet? Puccio demanded with a rhetorical air. Schrallhammer pondered one moment, then she replied evenly, "I was not concerned about the syringe and insulin. I didn't know it was so significant until later when the doctors alerted me to the dangers of insulin."

Zam!

Was she now saying that there was another bottle in the bag of which she had never spoken before? Puccio countered. The maid shot back, "That's not a new bottle. You misstate me, Mr. Puccio."

Puccio, shaken, then continued his gunfire (hoping to recoup) on Schrallhammer's earlier testimony that she had made notes of the label on the vials she found in the bag. He asked, "Didn't you tell Mr. Kuh that the labels were scraped off?"

"Mr. Puccio, if the labels were scraped off, how could I have written it down?"

Caught flatfooted by the witness's put-down question

back, Puccio gallantly emitted, "Good point," in a softened, if chastened, voice and proceeded to what he prayed would be a more fruitful subject. He realized that with this Teutonic witness he had reached a dead end on this point. Puccio wisely shifted to a different line of questioning, to defuse the focus he had inadvertently directed at the insulin in the black bag, the prosecution's "smoking gun."

MAXIM VIII

Woo the Jurors

Never forget on cross-examination that we are really addressing the minds and feelings of the jurors, wooing them all the time. Wooing, however, should never descend to fawning. A cross-examiner's manner should be that of a friend helping the jurors through their inquiry, never that of a gladiator striving for victory and looking down upon them as mere agents for winning. No one appears to have accomplished this sensitive relationship with the jury better than Harold R. Medina, whose uncanny success with jurors earned him admiration from the trial bar as one of the best in the field. He is now the senior judge of the United States Court of Appeals for the Second Circuit.

How many times have we sat through a presentation, a classroom lecture, or a sermon and found ourselves lost in our own thoughts? Probably more often than we would care to admit. Having grown up with television, most of us are conditioned to receive our information in thirty-second segments. A good cross-examiner must be sensitive to this. He must be aware that jurors may not always be interested in what is happening in court.

It is important therefore that the lawyer establish sensitive communication with the jury. Such communication entails more than just talking *at* the jury. Communication means that the lawyer has to build a sincere bridge between himself and the jury. He must allow the jury to relate to him as a person. He gets to know them at the outset on jury selection (voir dire). Lord help him should he choose to ignore them or act superior.

Too often lawyers view the practice of law as a cold, abstract, and logical exercise; they forget how, ultimately, law involves human beings. With unremembered exceptions, each juror wants to be fair and do justice. Treat the jury as doubting friends who really do want to know the truth and bring in the right (and fair) verdict.

MAXIM IX

Paint the Witness, Not Yourself, into a Corner

A married woman sued a stockbroker for the return of certain securities in the broker's possession to which she claimed title. Her husband testified that he had given the securities to the stockbroker as collateral against his own market speculations, but that they did not belong to him and, acting for himself and not as agent for his wife, he had taken her securities without her knowledge.

Joseph H. Choate, a famous cross-examiner in the old tradition, contended that if the securities belonged to the wife, she had either consented to her husband's use of the securities or was a partner with him in the transaction. Both contentions were flatly denied by the husband. During cross-examination of the husband, the following interchange took place:

CHOATE: When you ventured into the realm of speculations in Wall Street, I presume you contemplated the possibility of the market going against you, did you not?

WITNESS: [*putting down Choate*] Well, no, Mr. Choate, I went into Wall Street to make money, not to lose it. [*laughter in the courtroom*]

CHOATE: [*recovering*] Quite so, sir; but you will admit, will you not, that sometimes the stock market goes contrary to expectations?

WITNESS: Oh, yes, I suppose it does.

CHOATE: You say the bonds were not your own property, but your wife's.

WITNESS: Yes, sir.

CHOATE: And you say that she did not lend them to you for purposes of speculation, or even know you had possession of them?

WITNESS: Yes, sir.

CHOATE: You even admit that when you deposited the bonds with your broker as collateral against your stock speculations, you did not acquaint him with the fact that they were not your own property?

WITNESS: I did not mention whose property they were, sir.

CHOATE: *Well, sir, in the event of the market going against you and your collateral being sold to meet your losses, whom did you intend to cheat, your broker or your wife?*

Choate had painted the husband into a corner.

Sometimes focused, persistent cross-examination can eliminate physically the key adverse witness. The witness is painted into a corner and drops precipitously into the floor below. There was a recent case of national interest involving the alleged incompetent rating of a major public company (the Pennsylvania Railroad) that suddenly went bankrupt, leaving commercial paper investors out in the cold. The well-known rating company held itself out as expert and sold its rating service nationwide to investors. The director of the rating company on which buyers of securities relied had published an optimistic "prime" rating report for the railroad company right up to the last moment, when it suddenly disappeared from the screen into insolvency.

Trial counsel for the hoodwinked investors sought to show that the rating director was never competent to evaluate this railroad's financial health, and its rosy rating of "prime" to the dying day was tantamount to gross negligence, if not fraud.

The rating director himself was called to the witness stand on direct and subsequently cross-examined by the investors' trial counsel as follows:

INVESTORS' TRIAL COUNSEL: You mentioned that you were told by an officer of the rated railroad company it was going to raise some money by public offering?
RATING COMPANY'S DIRECTOR: That's right, sir.
Q. Did you make any inquiry about how that was coming along?
A. From whom, sir?
Q. From anyone.
A. No, I did not, sir, at the time.
Q. Did it come to your attention that that the rated company's underwriting was aborted?
A. Yes, it had, sir.
Q. When?
A. I don't remember the exact date. The latter part of May.
Q. Whom did you talk to?
A. The vice president, Mr. M.
Q. What did he say to you?
A. He told me that the underwriter was not going to go out with the issue.
Q. Did he say why?
A. Because they felt that the underwriter could not sell it.
Q. Did he say why they could not sell it?
A. No, he did not, sir.
Q. Anything to do with the financial condition of the rated corporation?
A. I can't answer for the underwriter, sir.

Q. Did you ask him a question about that?
A. No, I did not, sir.
Q. Did you ask him any questions whatever with regard to the ability of the corporation to raise funds?
A. No, I did not, sir.
Q. Did you think that that was important, whether they could raise funds at this time?
A. It was significant.
Q. Was it important?
A. Yes, it was.
Q. You didn't ask?
A. No, I did not, sir.

* * *

Q. When did it first come to your attention that the securities were not being honored by the company?
A. I have no knowledge of that.
Q. Do you have any knowledge today?
A. No, sir.
Q. Did you ever make any inquiry about it?
A. No.
THE JUDGE: [*incredulous tone*] Are you serious that you have no knowledge that these securities have not been paid by the rated company? Are you swearing under oath to that?
THE WITNESS: [*looking down*] We have nothing to do with the market. . . .
THE JUDGE: [*severely*] That isn't what was asked of you. You are under oath here as a witness. You were asked a question whether or not you knew whether the

company, the issuer of the securities, had made payment. *I believe your answer was you have no knowledge.*

THE WITNESS: [*very weak*] That is correct.

THE JUDGE: You are head of the rating division. . . . and you are saying in terms of your obligation to your company and to other persons, insofar as you may have any, you are not aware that the notes have in fact not been paid?

THE WITNESS: No, I am not.

THE JUDGE: I would say that is common knowledge of the person that has the slightest familiarity with [the rated corporation]. You were a witness in another case in this court?

THE WITNESS: Yes.

THE JUDGE: Do you know what that case was about?

THE WITNESS: Not completely, no, sir.

THE JUDGE: [*disgusted*] I think we will take recess.

* * *

Dogged persistence had resulted in showing the court the fact that the prime rating of the railroad company up to the time it dropped into bankruptcy was due to less than thorough investigation by the rating company's director. After this cross-examination by counsel and the judge, the witness never returned to the courtroom to complete his testimony, and the lawsuit by the investors against the rating company was handsomely settled forthwith.

Paint the witness, not yourself, into a corner. Often the judge comes in with gusto to prevent any escape.

MAXIM X

Avoid Asking One Question Too Many

There is a story about a cross-examiner who discovered that a witness had been confined in an insanity ward at one time and who sought with great delight to bring this out in order to shatter the witness's credibility.

The cross-examiner moved in with a smirky smile, and said, "Now, sir, would you tell the jury how you came to be confined in an asylum on Ward's Island?"

After a moment's silence the witness replied, "I was sent there because I was insane. You see, my wife was very ill with locomotor ataxia. She had been ill a year. I was her only nurse; I tended her night and day. We loved each other dearly. I was greatly worried over her long illness and frightful suffering. The result was I worried too deeply. She had been very good to me. I overstrained myself, and my mind gave way, but I am better now, thank you."

* * *

An art expert with an unusual second career was on the witness stand for cross-examination in which the plaintiff's counsel was intent on destroying the defendant's credibility. The case in Supreme Court, Suffolk County, involved evaluation of a fine painting which the plaintiff wished to donate, at high value, to a museum.

The defendant, who had English background and wit, did not share the plaintiff's optimism as to either the authenticity or value of the painting. A summary of the cross-examination follows:

Q. [*triumphantly*] Mr. Hildesley, do you have a second career?
A. Yes.
Q. [*with a simper*] Does this work take you on numerous occasions into private apartments on the Upper East Side for periods of approximately half an hour?
A. Yes.
Q. [*bearing in*] Do you work late at night?
A. Often.
Q. Does this job involve frequent activity on Saturdays and Sundays?
A. Yes.
Q. Do you have a wife?
A. Certainly.
Q. [*glancing at jury*] Does she ever accompany you on these visits?
A. Never.
Q. Would you like to tell the court and the jury what this alternative activity is?
A. With pleasure; I'm an Episcopal priest!

* * *

At the fourth Abscam trial in federal court in Brooklyn, twelve jurors and four alternates listened attentively to the big moment as defense counsel cross-examined the prosecution's main undercover witness, Melvin Weinberg. Weinberg was a convicted swindler who had worked with the federal agents to produce evidence against the defendants. The issue was entrapment.

"Define scam," demanded defense counsel James Pascarella, his voice loud as he cross-examined Weinberg.

Weinberg hesitated, then replied, "Where you try to pull something over on someone."

His voice rising, and approaching close to the witness, Pascarella shouted, "And isn't that *exactly* what you were doing in this case?"

Silence. The jury looked to the witness for his response. Weinberg calmly replied, "We were just trying to catch crooks."

Conviction soon followed.

* * *

One day I was assigned to prosecute a ring of interstate thieves in New York's garment district. The principal witness for the prosecution was the manager of a coat factory in Manhattan. It was crucial to the government's prosecution to show that the fur coats found in the trucks of the alleged thieves outside New York State had been stolen from the manager's factory. After direct testimony the manager was cross-examined by the defendant's lawyer. This veteran litigator was confident that he would destroy the manager's testimony that his company had made the coats in New York.

In bang-bang style, defense counsel picked up the box containing the fur coats, opened it, dramatically took out a coat, and shouted at the manager, "Thousands of these kinds of coats are made throughout the United States, aren't they? What's so unique about a white coat with a rabbit fur collar? What's so special about four buttons in front and standard needlework throughout?" He then approached the manager and screamed, "Here, take this coat, look this jury in the eye, and tell me that you cannot swear under oath that this very coat in your hands was made in your factory."

The manager stood up, cradling the coat in his arms. He peered down at it, looked up at the jury, and with a trace of mist in his eyes replied, "Don't a father know his own child?"

Again the deadly question back. The defendant pleaded guilty at this point, and the trial ended.

MAXIM XI

Don't Be Indignant

Judge Learned Hand came down to the U.S. attorney's office one day to talk to some young prosecutors to give us the word from a man who knew. In the course of his wise advice, he said, "When you come up to the court of appeals, it is all right for you once in a while to *act* indignant." Then he shouted, eyebrows flopping with the shake of his large head, "But never *be* indignant." I think this wisdom applies as well to the trial court, and particularly to cross-examination.

Don't *be* indignant! It will destroy your objectivity and judgment under fire.

Keep in mind the wisdom expressed by Clifford Mortimer, the late British barrister, father of the author John

Mortimer, that "the secret of cross-examination is not to examine crossly."

Last summer public television carried live the questioning of Associate Justice William H. Rehnquist by members of the Senate Judiciary Committee. Several senators were hostile in their questioning and in their choice of subject matter. Mr. Justice Rehnquist, a bright and sophisticated jurist, was wise and nimble in responding to a long and publicly displayed inquisition. He seldom gave ground and many times he made the attacking senators appear unprepared and off the mark. He never became arrogant under fire and never lost his cool. His was a memorable performance given little credit in the media. But here we saw—live—what actually happened, like a tennis match, back and forth, question and answer. Here was, considering the stakes and innuendo of politics, first-class theater. The consequence: either Rehnquist would be confirmed by the Senate and become chief justice of the United States Supreme Court or he would remain a powerful incisive associate justice for life.

As a segment of his effort to discredit or destroy Rehnquist, Senator Edward Kennedy chose to confront him with recent revelations that two houses Rehnquist had bought contained restrictive covenants, one barring sale to "any member of the Hebrew race" and the other to "any person not of the white or Caucasian race."

Mr. Justice Rehnquist, in reply, calmly labeled the restrictions "obnoxious," testified he never knew of them before recent disclosure, and—significantly—declared that such restrictive covenants have been legally unenforceable since the 1940s. The official transcript of the hearing of 31 July 1986 shows Senator Kennedy, riveted to an apparent FBI memorandum, fumbling to knock Rehnquist out of the box. The transcript does not reveal, however, the bewilderment of the witness as to Kennedy's rather clumsy efforts to block his promotion to chief justice:

SENATOR EDWARD M. KENNEDY [Democrat, Massachusetts]: Justice, the Senator from Vermont brought up some questions yesterday about the restrictive covenants in certain titles. The FBI report indicates that also on October 24, 1961, you obtained a title to Lot 3, which is in Palm Croft subdivision in Phoenix, Arizona. Are you familiar with that?

A. Certainly we owned property . . . we owned the home in Palm Croft, Arizona, from about 19—.

Q. Well, did you buy it in 1961?

A. Yes, that sounds right.

Q. And October 24 sounds about the time?

A. That sounds right.

Q. Do you still own that?

A. No.

Q. You sold it. When did you sell it?

A. I believe early in 1969.

Q. I see. On that particular provision is a report by Mrs. Gladys Cavette, who is the customer service department, Arizona Title Company, advised that that further research of the records by the title company revealed a warranty, Deed No. 328623, dated July 30, 1928, relating to Lot 3 of the Palm Croft subdivision, and the Article 11 of the warranty deed, is as follows: "No lot nor any part thereof within a period of ninety-nine years from the date of filing of the record on the plot of Palm Croft shall ever be sold, transferred or leased to, nor shall any lot be a part thereof within said period be inhabited by or occupied by any person not of the white or Caucasian race." Were you familiar with that particular provision?

A. I certainly don't recall it, no.

Q. Well, would you have read through the various . . . warranty deed on . . . you bought the land. Do you have any recollection? It's a long time ago, but . . .

A. It's 1961. I simply can't answer that, Senator. It was a title company transaction, I think, and one relies on the title company for the sufficiency of the deed. I simply can't answer whether I read through the deed or not.

Q. But you have no knowledge whether in that warranty . . . you didn't examine the warranty about any restrictions on the property?

A. I certainly have no recollection of it.

Q. Would you now examine the warranty if you purchased property today?

A. Well, if a lawyer were handling the thing for me . . . or any sort of a complicated warranty. . . . I think I would tend to rely on the lawyer.

Q. Even when you're familiar that there were those kinds of restrictions in many parts of the country, I expect, even in my own part, with regards to either Caucasians, whites or blacks or Jews?

A. Your question is would I examine a warranty deed now?
Q. Yes, to see if there's any restriction. Would you care if you joined a country club or something like that that restricted women or Jews.
A. No, certainly not.
Q. Or blacks?
A. No.
Q. Well, you'd know about that then. You would find out about that before you made application I assume.
A. Yes, I would.
Q. Well, would you check and see if there were any restrictions in terms of the purchase of that property.
A. Oh, in terms of . . . yes, I think I would.
Q. Well, when . . . you didn't before evidently. You didn't in 1961.
A. It simply hadn't occurred to me.
Q. Well, when did it start occurring to you?
A. Well, the discussion today or last evening has certainly brought it up.
Q. Well, you don't think that you should have before or any time? You don't think you should have before today, before yesterday?
A. Well, I must say my normal approach in looking at a statement of title was, you know does it convey good title and that sort of thing. I certainly not only thought but knew that this sort of a covenant is totally unenforceable and had been for years. Since the Supreme Court decision a long time ago. So, while very offensive, it has no legal effect.

Q. Well, did you sign the deed of transfer when you sold the property?

A. I'm sure I must have.

Q. Was the restriction still in it then?

Q. I can't answer from my own knowledge, but I certainly . . . we had done nothing to remove it as I recall in the years we . . . I would think it probably was.

SENATOR ORRIN G. HATCH [Republican, Utah]: This is the biggest red herring I've seen in the whole hearing, and there are a number of them. It's this business of these titles. He didn't know about it, he found out about it through this process. It's good that he has. Under *Shelley* v. *Kramer*, everybody in the world who understands constitutional law knows that these provisions are unconstitutional, may not be enforced by the courts in this country.

I just wonder if I could ask my two colleagues from Arizona and from Vermont if they'd just ask the public officials to strip those deeds of those provisions and let's just get rid of them, or I suppose you could go to a quit-claim process and just get them stripped off.

As I understand it he said he didn't know about them, he's going to take them off. I think it's ridiculous to make a big brouhaha about something this ridiculous.

It is ridiculous. Well, of course it's ridiculous. You know it's ridiculous. I know it's ridiculous. It isn't enforceable. Come on [*voices*]

SENATOR STROM THURMOND [Republican, South Carolina, the committee chairman]: Senator Hatch has the floor.

SENATOR HATCH: My gosh, you're jumping on every little possible detail you can. Let's be honest about it. I don't know a lawyer alive who goes through a house closing who reads every one of those documents if he's got another lawyer doing it for him. I never have. I don't think you have.

SENATOR KENNEDY: If the Senator will just yield on that point. I think part of the question is that this nominee was an official of the Justice Department, the Justice Department of the United States. In 1969 when he transferred a property that had that kind of restrictive provision in it. And I think that [*voices*] transfers a home who has not that particular responsibility.

SENATOR THURMOND: I might make this statement. We've had numbers of nominees here that have been involved this way. They bought property and did not realize it had certain restrictions. But whether it had restrictions or not, they aren't enforceable and they don't amount to anything and that's all been acknowledged so why waste more time.

SENATOR DENNIS DECONCINI [Democrat, Arizona]: I wonder how many of us on this committee could say that we have never owned a piece of property, either in trust or in escrow or in our names, that we have looked at every piece of the title. Maybe the Senator from Ohio can say that.

SENATOR KENNEDY: I think the point has to be made is the real question of the sensitivity of this nominee. The issue of civil rights.

A few days later, the newspapers reported that Senator Kennedy's brother John, when president, owned a house in Georgetown, Washington, D.C., that had a restrictive covenant not dissimilar to the subject matter of his inquiry of Mr. Rehnquist. The lesson is to proceed on questions that don't raise straw men and be sure your own skirts are clean on the point of your indignation.

MAXIM XII

Plan and Replan Your Sequence

The sequence in which cross-examination is conducted can be particularly important with a perjuring witness. Never put the ultimate important question until a proper foundation for it has been laid, even though that may take some time. When the adverse witness is then confronted with the circumstances, he can neither deny nor explain. (Trial lawyer Jack Swords made this technique an art form—often using it mercilessly on his associates in everyday conversation.) Damaging documents that could dramatically betray the witness's falsehoods often lose all steam and fall flat merely because they are handled in an unskilled way by neglect of building a proper foundation in advance.

At another point in prosecutor Murphy's cross-examination of psychiatrist Binger in the Alger Hiss perjury case, Murphy set out to show that it was really impossible for Dr. Binger to determine Whittaker Chambers's "psychopathic personality" from the content of the hypothetical question put to him as an "expert" during his direct testimony. Murphy's strategy involved the painstaking work of laying the foundation for undermining Dr. Binger's conclusion, building with facts, individually perhaps insignificant, but cumulatively destroying Dr. Binger's "expert" opinion.

PROSECUTOR MURPHY: Do you agree, Doctor, with the statement by a doctor who said, "To be sure, psychiatric investigation takes into consideration all bodily abnormalities of form and function, and no examination would be regarded as complete without careful physical studies as well?" Do you agree with that?

DR. BINGER: As regards patients who are to be treated, yes.

Q. With regard to giving testimony in court, no?

A. In the case of psychopathic personality there are one or two physical facts that are important.

Q. Doctor, some doctor said this and I am trying to find out whether you agree with him: "To be sure, psychiatric investigation takes into consideration all bodily abnormalities of form and function, and no examination would be regarded as complete without careful physical studies as well." Don't you agree with that, Doctor?

A. Certainly as regards patients.

Q. You said it yourself, didn't you?

A. [*weakly*] I don't recall. I have said an awful lot in my day.

Q. Now, Doctor, when you started to describe the different symptoms of a person with a psychopathic personality, you ran through twelve or so, and you said chronic, persistent, and repetitive lying; stealing; deception; alcoholism, and drug addiction; abnormal sexuality; vagabondage; panhandling. For our purposes, Doctor, we can eliminate immediately three of those, can't we—drug addiction, alcoholism, and sexual abnormality? There is nothing in the hypothetical question that you have that even touches on any of those?

A. That is right.

Q. Right. The first one I think you talked about when you started to outline the characteristics was the repetitive lying pattern. Doctor, do people who lie necessarily give to a psychiatrist a symptom of a psychopathic personality just by lying?

A. [*drifting away from a direct response*] Well, I have a case in mind of a patient—

Q. [*controlling the witness*] I have a number, too. But can you tell me generally, Doctor, whether people who lie, just that abstract thing . . . would that indicate to a trained psychiatrist that that person has one of the symptoms of a psychopathic personality?

A. Obviously not one lie, but a history of repetitive lying over twenty-five years or so would be evidence in the direction of that diagnosis.

Q. In other words, one lie by itself would mean nothing to you as a trained psychiatrist?

A. Isolated lie, isolated any event would mean nothing.

Q. Any event would mean nothing?

A. If it were isolated from the rest of the behavior.

Q. What would that indicate, Doctor, an occasional lie to

your wife as to whether you actually worked that night or didn't?

A. What would that indicate?

Q. Would it indicate a symptom of a psychopathic personality?

A. I wouldn't say so.

Q. You wouldn't think so.

A. No.

Q. Let us suppose, Doctor, a taxpayer lied a little bit in his income tax return on his contributions or expenses. What do you think that would indicate? A symptom of psychopathic personality?

A. It could; not necessarily.

Q. It could? It could indicate a symptom?

A. It could indicate a symptom. There would be an awful lot of psychopaths if that were the criterion.

Q. Supposing, Doctor, you were stopped by a policeman who said that you were speeding; you told him that you had a hurry call for a patient, had to get there by a certain time, and you lied a little bit, and you ended up with no ticket. Would that indicate a symptom of a psychopathic personality?

A. Certainly not.

Q. Well, let us suppose that some of us tell our children that there is a Santa Claus and continue that statement to children over a period of years until they are adolescent. Would you say that that indicates on the part of the parents a symptom of psychopathic personality?

A. No, I wouldn't.

Q. Would you say that telling the children for many,

many years that the stork brings the baby—would that indicate that the parent perhaps was manifesting a symptom of psychopathic personality?

A. Well, if the parents believed it, I would think it might.

Q. You think if a parent told his child that the child was brought by a stork, and that that parent, talking to his or her child, believed it, that that would be only a psychopathic personality symptom?

A. Oh, no; it would be a symptom of much else.

Q. You said it. I am talking, Doctor, about psychopathic personalities, and I am trying to develop what you mean when you talk about the symptoms of lying; and doesn't it come down to this, Doctor, that . . . but if there is a *purpose,* that it is not a symptom at all?

A. Not at all.

Q. Not at all?

A. No. Psychopaths usually have a purpose when they lie.

Q. Yes, but is it a real purpose?

A. Well, it may be a real purpose; it may be a fantasy; it may be very real; it may be to accomplish the destruction of somebody or something.

Q. Well, tell us, Doctor, the purpose of a parent telling a child that Santa Claus comes at Christmas—why is that not a psychopathic symptom? The parent has a purpose.

A. That is an accepted piece of folk mythology, and parents simply take on what is traditional; it has no malign purpose.

Q. It has no malign purpose?

A. No.

Q. The purpose has to be malign in order to come within a psychopathic personality symptom?

A. It does not have to be. It often is.

Q. It often is? How about lying to your wife to avoid an unpleasant argument?

A. Pretty normal.

Q. Normal?

A. Pretty normal performance.

Q. Some lying is normal, Doctor?

A. In the sense of statistically normal, yes. It is undesirable, I think.

Q. But it has a purpose. Doctor, wouldn't you say that lying to your wife rather than to have an argument about something that is inconsequential is not a psychopathic symptom?

A. Is not?

Q. Is not.

A. Well, you would have to give me the example of what kind of lie and under what circumstances. You don't make a diagnosis on the basis of an isolated episode.

Q. In other words, Doctor, don't you have to know what is behind the reason for the lie in order to form an opinion, as a doctor?

A. Unless there is a consistent habit of untruth.

Q. Yes, but consistent with a purpose, Doctor? Let us suppose it is consistent with a purpose.

A. That doesn't matter. It doesn't change it.

Q. Let us suppose, Doctor, that you were captured in the last war, and you were constantly being plagued in violation of all of the treaties and asked questions beyond your name and rank, and so forth, asked where you were stationed, how many men were billeted with you, what you were doing, what the troops were doing, what they had done last, and so forth, and you consistently told a story of the most outlandish lies for the purpose of deceiving your captors, would you say you were evidencing a symptom of psychopathic personality at that time?

A. No, I would not.

Q. Because you had a definite purpose in lying, isn't that correct, Doctor?

A. I was trying to save me—

Q. Not even malign?

A. That is right.

Q. But you had a specific purpose in mind, the purpose of deceiving your captors?

A. That is right.

Q. And, of course, not disclosing the trust or violating the trust that they had placed in you as an officer; that would not be psychopathic lying?

A. It could be but it does not need to be.

Q. It does not need to be?

A. No.

Q. Doesn't it help, then, Doctor, in analyzing the symptoms to find out what the specific purpose was in lying so as to learn whether or not it is just the ordinary normal statistical lying, or something else?

A. [*finally giving in*] Yes, it would help.

* * *

Like any creative work, no single event or question stood out in prosecutor Murphy's examination. Rather, it was the effective weaving of individual facts, each with its own subtleties, that made his cross-examination so powerful. He succeeded in wearing down Dr. Binger and cumulatively undermining his conclusion that Whittaker Chambers, Alger Hiss's accusor, was a psychopathic liar. This feat alone brought about Alger Hiss's conviction for perjury and his downfall. One hundred hours of preparation for Dr. Binger's cross-examination. The trial of the century hung on that memorable cross-examination by prosecutor Thomas Murphy.

MAXIM XIII

Consider Timing

During the cross-examination, always look for a high peak (if there is one . . .) upon which to terminate and sit down. Keep an eye on the clock, because it is always best to finish a session strong and, in some cases, to have overnight for honing of further cross-examination. Try to have your best shot come just before you finish the day's session.

In his earlier testimony, Dr. Binger, in the Alger Hiss case, had testified that a "well-formulated habit of lying" was one of the significant factors he considered in concluding that Chambers was a psychopath. Murphy, using Binger's own testimony, succeeded in showing that Chambers did not have a "well-formulated habit of lying." Therefore, it followed that Binger's conclusion of

Chamber's psychological state was erroneous. Murphy led Binger through the facts until Binger finally agreed with him that it would not be accurate to say that Chambers had a "habit" of lying. Murphy, realizing that this was the highest point of this exchange, wisely asked for a recess, allowing Dr. Binger's damaging concession to sink in with the jury.

PROSECUTOR MURPHY: Doctor, I was trying to find out the number of lies that you had relied upon which caused you to say that the habit of lying had been well formulated by that time, and we were talking about the time in 1935 when the Breen application was made; and in order to be specific about it we had got, one, the high-school incident; two, the use of the name Charles Adams when as a boy after high school he ran away from home—and what is the next?

DR. BINGER: Well, he lied when he said he had not stolen books from the library at Columbia, whereas stolen books were found in his locker and in his home.

* * *

DR. BINGER: I think we have four [lies], have we not?

MR. MURPHY: Call it four, if you like.

A. I think those are four pretty significant lies.

Q. Would you say that a person who has made those four lies that you have described, evidences a habit of lying? Would you say that, Doctor, as an experienced doctor?

A. Well, "habit" may be too strong a word.

MR. MURPHY: Yes, I thought so. [*again he stops at a peak*]

I have run over the usual time for adjournment, Your Honor.

THE COURT: We will adjourn until a quarter past two.

* * *

Consider your timing, and finish on a high note.

MAXIM XIV

Avoid Flip Remarks

Francis L. Wellman tells about an interchange at the end of a long but unsuccessful cross-examination by an experienced trial lawyer. The lawyer remarked rather testily to the witness, "Well, Mr. Wittemore, you have contrived to manage your case pretty well."

"Thank you, Counselor," replied the witness with a twinkle in his eye. "Perhaps I might return the compliment if I were not testifying under oath."

A witness is perhaps well advised to answer a hostile question in one of three ways: yes, no, or a smile.

While avoiding flip answers of flip questions is, on balance, sound advice, I'm often amazed at someone violating this rule of experience and getting away with it. One example is William F. Buckley, Jr., enfant terrible and editor of the *National Review.* I first met him in the early 1940s at the dinner table of his family's house in Sharon, Connecticut, where his father made him sit next to him at the long table to protect him from physical harm from his brothers and sisters. Buckley was about fifteen years old. He taunted them as the youngest and most precocious child and they sought instant revenge for his acerbic, stinging wit randomly directed at them.

These scenes from forty-five years ago were recollected recently when Mr. Buckley appeared as a witness in federal court in the District of Columbia in a rough-and-tumble libel suit and countersuit between the conservative Liberty Lobby (represented by gung ho Mark Lane) and the *National Review* (represented by J. Daniel Mahoney). Irrepressible is the only word for Buckley's performance, flippant to the nth degree in thrusting, riposting clashes with Mark Lane, no uninhibited neophyte himself. The judge, Joyce Hens Green, had her hands full. When questioned by his nemesis, Lane, Buckley felt claustrophobic because *he* was being asked questions.

"Am I allowed to ask a question, Your Honor?" Buckley says benignly.

"No, no, no," replies the judge. "It's a one-way street, Mr. Buckley."

Buckley emits, "Sorry." Then, later, unreformable Buckley pleads to the judge, "Your Honor, when he [Mark Lane] asks a ludicrous question, how am I supposed to behave?" Again to Mark Lane, Buckley exclaims, "I decline to answer that question; it's too stupid." Lane blanches and his exasperation mounts. Lane makes a series of interminable objections to Buckley's feathery answers. Buckley sighs audibly, "I'm terribly constipated by these constant interruptions." Mark Lane looks at the judge, eyes imploring. Then Lane asks Buckley what were his duties as a young man at the Central Intelligence Agency (CIA). Buckley solemnly refers to his job-secrecy and replies with a wide grin: "None of your business." Later Lane charges that the *National Review* had argued that "militant sex deviates" should have the "right to molest your children." Buckley looks at Lane: "Are you sure you have the date straight?" Quick smile from Buckley to Lane and the judge.

Buckley's lawyer defended his flippancy as a long and windy fight for a principle—the integrity of the real conservative movement. The suit cost Buckley $160,000, which went to Buckley's law firm, Windels, Marx, Davies & Ives. "No relation, Marx," shrugged Buckley, having as always, even as in the early days in Sharon, the last word in any confrontation.

* * *

John F. Kennedy answered questions with great skill and charm at the first televised presidential news conference in 1961. He was forty-three years old; today he would be sixty-nine. Russell Baker, after the news conference, declared Kennedy "a new star with a tremendous national appeal, the skill of a consummate showman." Kennedy never seemed in these encounters to descend to flip remarks. He relied instead on his black-belt rapier Irish wit. Presidential news conferences have never been the same since.

A year earlier, serious-minded President Dwight Eisenhower surprised his White House press conference when a reporter asked for just one "major idea" instigated by his vice president, Richard Nixon. Eisenhower responded: "If you give me a week, I might think of one. I don't remember."

Bad.

MAXIM XV

Let the Con Man Run You Ragged

Sometimes an adverse witness is so full of con, so cunning, knowledgeable, so willing to dart and weave, that the cross-examiner has to exercise more than the usual amount of patience.

One such witness was Ronald Earl Gates, a Far Eastern manager for P. F. Collier, Inc., purveyors of encyclopedias. Gates was suspected of defrauding the company by falsely treating full cash payments for sets of encyclopedias as installments only in reporting his accounting to the home office on Long Island, New York—somewhat of a Ponzi operation. But proof was scanty. Gates had his headquarters in Tokyo, but his territory extended down to Australia. He was married to a Japanese lady and spoke fluent Japanese, and most of his employees were Japanese.

Wishing to avoid serpentine Japanese court procedures, when word came that Gates was in Australia, I flew to Sydney with a draft of summons and complaint. Gates was served in a suit for fraud, accounting, and breach of fiduciary duty in the Australian courts. Then, after retaining a barrister, I went to Tokyo. The Japanese police commissioner, after a conference over green tea, agreed to open a criminal investigation of Gates. With luck I got hold of the original books of account and placed them in safekeeping. They constituted Exhibit A for the conviction of Gates for civil and criminal fraud. We obtained an injunction and an attachment in the Tokyo courts against Gates and his property. The meticulous police methodically placed red stickers on everything he owned.

No sooner had the criminal investigation commenced than Gates and his wife fled Japan for Hawaii, where Gates brazenly induced the former attorney general of Hawaii, Shiro Kashiwa, to bring an action *against* Collier for commissions and accounting. Gates's case was sufficiently credible that a countersuit for fraud had to be a bull's-eye.

The five-week case was tried before Federal Judge Martin Pence in Honolulu. Gates had made a fool of me in four days of pretrial depositions by nonanswers, flippancies, declaring no knowledge or recollection when plainly untrue, and by irrelevant speeches for the record. Then, during cross-examination at the trial, cocky as ever, he took the same tack—dodging, weaving, evading. Judge Pence was not amused. He gave the decision from the bench against Gates and for Collier on counterclaims and wrote a decision* in which the court stated:

> Gates took the stand and his hesitancy to answer defendant's and the court's questions, his nervousness, his constant wetting of lips, his reluctance to make any positive statement under cross-examination, his repudiation of his own signature

* Reported at 256 F.Supp.204.

until it was conclusively proved to him that he had signed certain documents, his loss of memory regarding transactions until the documents signed by him covering the transactions were presented to him, his denial of facts and events until written proof was shown to him, his steady and repeated equivocal answers to direct questions all lead the court to give little credit to anything he testified to unless corroborated by other and more trustworthy proof. . . . The court fully believes . . . Gates ordered these ledgers set up as they were for the specific purpose of obtaining ready cash—by falsely and fraudulently changing the COD and cash orders into term orders and keeping all of the cash for his own use until each term payment became due.

Gates appealed to the Ninth Circuit Court of Appeals—unsuccessfully—and then twice by petition tried to obtain the interest of the United States Supreme Court. In the meantime we had persuaded the United States attorney in the Eastern District of New York to indict Gates for mail fraud. Gates finally pleaded guilty and was sentenced to three years in jail.

On the bail motion after his plea of guilty, we advised the court that Gates had two previous convictions for petty larceny. "Oh," Gates's counsel interposed to Judge Walter Bruckheusen, "at the time of those convictions he was only an infant."

The court asked, "How old *was* he?"

Gates's counsel answered, "Twenty years, Your Honor", to which the judge replied, "Well, *some infant!*" and set high bail. Gates entered prison at that point.

* * *

Another example of cross-examining lawyers' patient strategy that brought tragedy and stiff jail sentences for the opposition: you may have followed the case of the Securities and Exchange Commission (SEC) against former Deputy Secretary of Defense Paul Thayer, accusing him of insider trading while he was the powerful head of a large aviation-oriented corporation LTV. In January 1984, Thayer—protesting indignantly his absolute innocence—resigned his government office in a letter to President Reagan in order to defend against charges he illegally shared inside information about his company's corporate decisions that affected stock-market prices with some friends including his flamboyant Dallas broker, Billy Bob Harris, and—as it turned out—his girlfriend on the side, attractive brunette Sandra Ryno. These friends of Thayer obtained large profits from stock-market information the general public did not have. The SEC would soon refer the evidence to the Justice Department for investigation on possible allegations of fraud, obstruction of justice, and perjury. Charges of somewhat technical and vague securities law violation would ultimately balloon to grave, conspiratorial criminal charges.

Paul Thayer, former head of the United States Chamber of Commerce and one of America's top business executives, had strongly declared that the case was entirely "without merit" and that he had confidence that he would be fully exonerated. He wanted no part of any settlement or compromise. His lawyers echoed his forthright integrity and innocence.

Courthouse observers insist that the case could have been settled before any actual testimony was required with a compromise consent decree (i.e., neither admitting or denying guilt) and suitable monetary disgorgement of profits made by Thayer's friends. Thayer's stiff not-guilty-in-any-way stance led, months later, to a heavy prison sentence for him that stunned everyone. What happened?

Besides Thayer's arrogant cover-up, his undoing was largely due to a strategy of inquiry patiently pursued by the SEC investigation lawyers. Simply put, they allowed the friends of Thayer who had benefited from the inside information to run them ragged with lies, petty lies, and tall stories. Before long the house of cards fell, leaving Paul Thayer—humiliated and broken, a tragic figure—no choice at that point but to plead guilty to obstructing justice. There is no evidence that Thayer ever told his own trusting lawyers the truth.

A knowledgeable voluntary informer (yes, disgruntled) provided the SEC lawyers earlier with a strong lead as to the facts showing how the crime was committed. Depositions were taken first of Paul Thayer's friends who had benefited from inside information from him. The principal witness deposed was Billy Bob Harris, Thayer's nightlife pal, famous for his high life-style and generous parties. Understandably the friends involved wanted to protect Thayer—but here they went so far as to lie in spades.

Over a dozen of these lesser targets of the SEC investigation were represented by Dallas lawyer Joel Held, who although present at the perjured depositions, did not do anything visibly to preclude the gross misstatements under oath of his clients on the record.

The SEC lawyers, led by Assistant United States Attorney Charles Roistacher, had specific information about the details of wrongdoing and the close relationship between Paul Thayer and his girlfriend of six years, Sandra Ryno. The prosecutors artfully pretended ignorance of this critical evidence showing that Paul Thayer had actually discussed details of his inside information scheme with his broker Billy Bob Harris in the presence of girlfriend Sandra Ryno. Fearing a jail sentence was imminent for her when she learned from the investigators that a perjury net was encircling Thayer's "friends," she bolted the cover-up of Thayer's innocence of giving "inside information" on his corporation's activities. After she agreed to turn state's evidence there was no viable defense left for Paul Thayer.

When Paul Thayer finally pleaded guilty, he hoped to be saved from a prison sentence—the anxious last hope of all white-collar defendants. But an angry federal Judge Richey sentenced sixty-five-year old Paul Thayer, his distressed wife and daughter beside him, to four years in prison. His equally shaken broker, Harris, got the same sentence. Paul Thayer's conviction and ruin is due in large part to the tipped-off friends lying to the SEC about their knowledge of Paul Thayer's activities, while SEC lawyers listened calmly, saying to themselves: Let them ramble on; let them fabricate their hearts out; we can wait patiently until ready to spring the trap on their blatant perjury; then we'll have our ironclad case against one of the biggest fish ever caught violating the inside-trading securities laws. The irony is that, but for the lying, the case was disposable two years earlier by the SEC for what many believe would have been a mild consent judgment and fine.

Sometimes in cross-examination let the witness run you ragged. Be patient. The result can be startling.

MAXIM XVI

Witnesses Sometimes Brainwash Themselves

Sir John Romilly wrote in an old English opinion:

> It must always be borne in mind how extremely prone persons are to believe what they wish. It is a matter of frequent observation that persons dwelling for a long time on facts which they believed must have occurred, and trying to remember whether they did so or not, come at last to persuade themselves that they do actually recollect the occurrences of circumstances which at first they only begin by *believing* must have happened. What was originally the result of imagination becomes in time a result of recollection. Without imputing anything like willful and corrupt perjury to witnesses of this description they often in truth bonafide believe that they have heard and remembered conversations and observations which in truth never existed, but are the mere offspring of their imaginations.

In a recent book, *Vital Lies, Single Truths: The Psychology of Self-Deception,* Daniel Goleman describes a study done by the psychologist Ulric Neisser concerning John Dean's testimony of the crucial Watergate meeting he had with President Nixon on September 15, 1972.

Neisser found that a comparison of John Dean's testimony with the transcripts of the taped conversation showed great discrepancies, but concluded that John Dean was not lying. Rather, Dean was describing how he thought and hoped the events should have been.

This is a common experience. The mind develops certain blind spots in perception and memory, which allows us to cope with the unpleasant and threatening experiences we face. This mental blind spot can be found in social groupings as well, where people in a community commonly ignore certain realities without being aware of doing so. In cross-examining a witness we have to keep this tolerance in mind.

* * *

There is a popular tale about the American lawyer and his wife who were driving in Scotland several summers ago. They came upon a country courthouse with a number of automobiles parked outside. Typically, the lawyer said, "Let's go inside and see what's going on."

Inside the small paneled courtroom, they found what appeared to be a car-accident lawsuit in full swing. There was the judge in magisterial regalia with white wig. Below were counsel, also bewigged and posturing confidently. The plaintiff witness was being questioned by his counsel at the stand. Apparently the plaintiff was nervous under the questioning of his own lawyer. The judge rumbled and grew restive as the questioning stumbled along. Finally, the judge lost patience and interrupted plaintiff's counsel.

"Mr. Counselor," said the judge, peevishly, "doesn't

your client know the doctrine of *volenti non fit injuria* [he who consents cannot receive an injury]?"

The counselor below looked up at the judge and replied, "M'Lord, in the hills from which my client comes, they speak of little else."

MAXIM XVII

Size Up Your Witness

If the witness you are about to cross-examine has demonstrated that he is a good citizen, decent and unbiased, who testified to the basic facts and has not harmed your case in any essential way, what should you do? The answer is, don't cross-examine. If you do, it should be for a specific purpose, and that purpose should always be a significant material gain for your client's cause.

One of the great cross-examiners, Max Steuer, put it well:

> [In] my book cross-examination should be pointed to two objectives: either to destroy the story told by the witness or to destroy the witness himself. If neither of these objectives is attainable (and if you have properly prepared your case, you should know the prospect) a pointless and scoreless cross-examination does your case more harm than good. And when you have scored your point on cross-examination, for heaven's sake, quit.

Max Steuer's son, Aaron, a senior judge of the New York Supreme Court, Appellate Division, First Department, was for many years a trial judge. He died at eighty-seven in 1985 and the presiding justice of the Appellate Division, who served on the bench with Justice Steuer, said, "Judge Steuer had an intellect clear, formidable, and with a fine cutting edge that left no one in doubt of its elegance and power." His acidic criticism of awkward young lawyers became well known in the course of his judicial career. One day a young lawyer was cross-examining, going on and on without scoring. Finally, Justice Steuer leaned over the bench and breathed, "Young man, don't you know it is no shame to sit down?" I was the boy.

In a case involving a contested will, my partner Whitney North Seymour, Jr., was about to start his cross-examination of the lawyer who drafted an incompetent will when the judge interrupted, saying to the will-drafter lawyer on the stand:

COURT: Do you know what the liability here is for poor draftsmanship in this document . . . in New York State for a document of this kind? Do you know what *your* liability is?

WITNESS: [*hesitantly*] I would imagine grave.

COURT: Grave? No. I tell you very frankly I wish it were grave. The fact of the matter is that you can't be sued by anybody in this courtroom.

WITNESS: Thank you, I'm happy to hear that.

COURT: But if you were in the state of California, you would be hung.

WITNESS: Well, I'm not going to move to California.

When the judge finally finished with the witness, he

directed his attention to my partner and inquired, "Anything else? I don't think you started your cross."

SEYMOUR: I have finished, Your Honor.

Indeed, sometimes keeping your mouth shut can be the most effective manner of cross-examination.

MAXIM XVIII

Avoid Petty Points

What do you do when a witness on direct has lobbed a grenade into your case and scored a direct hit, and you know that you cannot effectively turn the witness around? At such times you should resist the temptation to bring out trivial inconsistencies in the direct testimony in the hope that they would discredit the witness and his story. That would amount to answering a strong argument with a weak one. The contrast will only make matters worse for your client. Rise, say firmly, "No questions." Get on with the case, your face unconcerned and free of redness.

The inept petty-point cross-examination of an expert witness called to testify in support of a fee for legal services in federal court in New York may have resulted in a jury bringing in a verdict for more than even sued for. The stunning result may be attributed in part to defense trial counsel descending to the use of petty points in his questioning instead of foregoing cross-examination unless he actually had in hand something of substance.

One day an experienced and conscientious lawyer, Perry Trafford, Jr., was retained by a prominent man, Harrison Lillibridge, and his family to establish their right to hold title to and sell real-estate property they claimed underneath Macy's department store on Herald Square. At their request, Trafford provided legal services for them for fifty-two months, resulting in the Lillibridge family receiving at a settlement closing $8,870,922.41. Following that bonanza, lawyer Trafford sent a modest bill to Mr. Lillibridge in the amount of $35,000, which was rejected out of hand. The Lillibridge family had no need, they said, for the services of Trafford or his firm and would not pay. Negotiations were fruitless. Trafford's firm was compelled to bring suit in federal court against Harrison Lillibridge, asking for $50,000 as the value of these legal services. Harrison Lillibridge was also a lawyer and a member of the New York bar.

At the trial before Judge Richard Levet and a jury, trial counsel for plaintiff Trafford called as an expert witness former chief judge of the New York Supreme Court Appellate Division, First Department, David W. Peck, a distinguished public servant and able trial lawyer. Judge Peck, now a senior partner at Sullivan & Cromwell in New York, testified on direct that in his opinion the value of the legal services of Trafford's firm was $60,000—$10,000 more than Trafford was asking of the jury.

Fire in his eyes, Orwell McKay, defense counsel for Harrison Lillibridge, rose mightily to cross-examine plaintiff's expert witness David W. Peck:

MCKAY: [*voice rising*] Mr. Peck, do you know Mr. Trafford?

PECK: No, I do not.

Q. [*thrusting finger at witness*] When did you meet him for the first time?

A. I haven't met him. I don't know him, I said.

Q. [*rambling*] Did you ever have any matter with Mr. Trafford?

A. No.

Q. Do you know whether or not Mr. Trafford is an experienced real-estate attorney?

A. I am so advised. . . .

Q. Do you know whether or not that firm has a reputation in the profession as a well-established and thoroughly experienced real-estate firm?

A. [*evenly*] I believe so. They have a reputation of being a good firm in general practice, and I have been informed that they have done a very considerable amount of real-estate work.

Q. Did you ever do any real-estate work with them?

A. No.

Q. Did you ever do any real-estate work with Mr. Trafford?

A. No.

Q. Did you have any occasion to hire their firm at any time?

A. No.

Q. [*repeating*] Did you have occasion to recommend their firm at any time?

A. No.

Q. If your firm had an important real-estate matter involving $9 million or $8 million, would you recommend Mr. Trafford?

A. Well, as I said, I personally don't know Mr. Trafford so I would not be likely to engage somebody that I do not know.

Q. Would you recommend his firm?

A. I would recommend his firm on the basis of what I have heard about the firm.

Q. Have you heard that his firm specializes in real estate?

A. I have been advised that real-estate and estate work are their concentration with general practice.

Q. From whom did you get your information?

A. [One of his partners] so informed me.

Q. You received your information from one of the members of the firm?

A. That's right.

Q. [*shifting to new field*] Now, Mr. Peck . . . you asked plaintiff's trial counsel before you were willing to express an opinion whether this time spent was partners' time or associates' time or junior partners' time?

A. Yes, I did ask.

Q. Does that make a difference?

A. Yes.

Q. Would you tell the jury what the difference is?

A. Well, a partner's time, a senior experienced lawyer, his time is worth more than a younger, less experienced lawyer, and on down the line, depending upon how experienced the associate is, senior or junior.

Q. And if a senior partner performs it, is it fair and reasonable for him to charge the client for what a junior could have performed?

A. I would say if it wasn't necessary or desirable for the partner to do it, that he should not charge the client for what could be more economically done by an associate, yes.

Q. [*wandering*] And does that apply to other categories, such as attending family meetings and meeting members of a family?

THE COURT: Attending family meetings?

Q. [*clarifying*] Attending family meetings during the process of negotiations.

THE COURT: And advising them on the law and other factors?

A. I should think that a partner who is in charge of a matter would be expected to do that.

Q. And would it be considered necessary for a partner to confer with a client in order to try to get the retainer, would that be considered preliminary to getting a client?

A. Well, I am not sure that I understand your question, Mr. McKay, but if you mean consultation with the client looking toward a possible retainer, if it is a small amount of work, I suppose that a lawyer would likely not charge for it at all, but if it is a substantial amount of work and leads to the retainer and is integrated into the whole service, he would charge for it, yes.

Q. And if a rather substantial part of the work was interviewing the client and other prospective clients, looking forward to the retainer, and that is included in the number of hours that were spent, would that affect your opinion?

A. No, it would not.

Q. It would not affect your opinion?

A. No.

Q. Even though that is work that you say in many circumstances would be without charge?

A. Well, I take it from your question this was a substantial amount of work that was done this way.

Q. Assume there was a substantial amount of work.

A. Then I would include it in the overall services and expect it to be charged for, the same as any other services.

Q. [*disappointed with the expert's answers*] *It wouldn't make any difference to you?*

A. [*firmly*] No.

That literally concluded the cross-examination of plaintiff's sole expert witness in support of Trafford's requested fee by Lillibridge's trial counsel. Shortly thereafter the jury brought in a verdict for Mr. Trafford's firm in an amount of $60,000—$10,000 more than demanded in the complaint and the exact figure given by plaintiff's expert David W. Peck as his opinion of the true worth of Mr. Trafford's legal services. The jury had obviously accepted the opinion of the expert Peck who had sustained, with flags flying, a pathetic cross-examination laced with petty points that went nowhere. No cross-examination of Peck at all would have been better strategy.

MAXIM XIX

Don't Give Up

If you consider the goal worthwhile, don't give up. Be as persistent as you can. Too often we see a cross-examiner go on to another subject after the witness on cross refuses to give a direct answer to a question. Rework your inquiries in different ways and insist on an answer.

The asbestos litigation which came into the limelight in the 1970s with juries awarding large sums of damages to insulation workers exposed to asbestos was the accumulation of more than fifteen years of painstaking investigations and numerous lawsuits. To the various lawyers involved in bringing suits against the asbestos manufacturers, it was a period of enormous frustration, losing case after case because they simply could not crack the manufacturers' and suppliers' state-of-the-art defense that they *knew* nothing of the ghastly danger of asbestos.

In a 1976 case against Johns-Manville, an asbestos-insulation manufacturer, the defense lawyers succeeded with its claim that Johns-Manville and other insulation manufacturers had no reason to know that asbestos insulators were at risk of developing asbestosis. There simply was nothing in terms of medical and scientific data, they argued, that could have warned and alerted the asbestos industry about the harmful effects of asbestos dust—at least until 1964, when Dr. Irving Selikoff at Mount Sinai Hospital made public his studies on asbestos.

The defense team had as their witness a well-known, sixty-year-old pathologist from Charleston, South Carolina, Dr. McIver. Dr. McIver testified that as practicing doctor he did not have any knowledge of the danger of asbestos until 1964. McIver was suave and persuasive, the credible grand old professor with tweeds and pipe.

Plaintiffs' lawyers realized the awful consequences of his testimony. Initial attempts to shake McIver's testimony through cross-examination proved futile. Instead of simply moving on, or terminating the cross-examination, the plaintiffs' lawyers made two crucial tactical mistakes. One, they persisted in questioning McIver aimlessly. This simply reenforced the image of McIver the *expert.* Two, they countered with calling their own expert witnesses, two young doctors—one of whom had been McIver's student. In retrospect these trial errors are apparent.

Cross-examination by defendants' lawyers, brought out that plaintiffs' two expert witnesses had not even started medical school when Dr. Selikoff conducted his famed study of asbestos.

It took the jury less than one hour to acquit defendant Johns-Manville, finding that it could not have known the dangers which asbestos posed.

This litigation took place in the early phases of the asbestos controversy. But the plaintiffs' lawyers refused to give up. They began in-depth sleuthing, which eventually uncovered stunning evidence (some of it found in the basement files of Newark Federal Courthouse) that the industry had known about the ravages of asbestos fiber as early as the 1920s. The subsequent litigations as we will see (Maxim XXV) took a violent turn, and major asbestos manufacturers sought protection in bankruptcy from an avalanche of successful and costly claims. After the first disappointing trials it would have been so easy to quit but plaintiffs' trial counsel refused to knuckle under and later turned the tide with irrefutable "smoking-gun" documents.

MAXIM XX

Startle with Silence: The Pin-Drop Effect

When the opposition witness during your cross has finally been coaxed or coerced into making a material admission that is important to your case, it is often effective to stop asking questions for a moment and let the response sink in with the jury. A moment of quiet in the courtroom can be startling, and in some cases it wakes up a juror or two. I call this the pin-drop effect.

MAXIM **XXI**

Let the Humanities Be Reflected in Your Cross-Examination

A cross-examiner in developing his or her skills should remember the importance of continuous education outside the law. When we consider the personality, knowledge, and character of great cross-examiners, a common factor is apparent: a broad educational background and a Theodore Roosevelt curiosity about everything. The accomplished cross-examiner is more likely a generalist than a specialist. Education outside of the law is an ongoing endeavor and should never stop.

In recent years many observers believe there has been a decline in the art of cross-examination. This downward trend might be linked to the decline in the importance of the liberal arts—history, English, literature, philosophy. The pressures of law school are so great that most students read nothing but law. The pressures of the law firm are so great that most lawyers, older and younger, concentrate on their legal specialty, whether in or out of the office. For economic reasons, many large law firms urge, if not coerce, young lawyers to specialize prematurely, a narrowing decision hard to rescind. This insidious practice reminds me of foot-binding in early China.

A recent Rockefeller Foundation study, *The Humanities in American Life,* credited the humanities with helping people make critical judgments. The report urged that *critical thinking* be reviewed as a basic skill.

Lucid critical thinking is an absolute basic of cross-examination—first, from the outset, when the witness is identified, then through preparation of the witness sheet, and again, especially, in the heat of the trial. No one can predict the consequences of the courtroom battle. "To ask a cross-examiner how he succeeds," Emory Buckner told the *Harvard Law Review,* "is to ask the artist . . . 'how do you mix paints?' "

Many now believe that broadly educated persons have training and practice to *think* more precisely, to understand the meaning of words and to *ask* the right questions to elicit facts on which the right decisions can be made. Despite the irritating banality of the advice and the whiff of elitism, it is worth taking to heart if we are to develop maximum skills for questioning.

Recently President Reagan was asked by a college student, "I'd like to know what you see as the value of a liberal-arts education in today's fast-moving, high-tech society?" Reagan replied, "Well, I have one myself, and I've been trying to figure out how it set me back."

Study of the arts and philosophy encourages the person to ask not only the more precise but also the *larger questions.* In conducting his cross-examination, the questioner must always keep his main objective in focus. This is true for most of us, lawyers and nonlawyers alike.

High-caliber critical thinking cannot evolve without strong doses of the liberal arts. Recently I talked with a Columbia law student who organized a literature club at which a selected book is discussed every two weeks.

That young man's grandfather followed the same course over his sixty years at the bar and was considered to be a master advocate and one of the best cross-examiners. He extrapolated the truth gently, often with a smile. He also had time to be president of the American Bar Association, the Association of the Bar of the City of New York, and the American College of Trial Lawyers. He grew up in a library.

A friend told me that on the day Franklin Delano Roosevelt was inaugurated president of the United States, he paid a courtesy call on a former justice of the Supreme Court, Oliver Wendell Holmes, Jr. Holmes was then ninety-two years old. The president discovered him in his library reading Plato. Roosevelt asked, "Why do you read Plato, Mr. Justice?" To which Holmes replied steadily, "To improve my mind, Mr. President."

MAXIM **XXII**

Your Questions Should Be Pithy, Uncharacterized, and Closed-Ended

Your questions should be short, definite, clear, pithy, without characterization, and closed-ended. Don't ask general questions that your witness can answer with a speech; this gives the hostile witness a chance to bring in testimony otherwise inadmissible and self-serving. You must *control* the opposition witness on cross-examination, or the witness will destroy the questioner and, in turn, his client's cause.

The opposite is true of course if the questioner has a friendly witness, such as a candidate for chief justice of the United States Supreme Court, and the questioner wishes, as many senators did at recent judiciary hearings in Washington, D.C., to give that witness an opportunity to expound upon his own self-serving views.

For the hostile witness, however, closed-ended or leading questions are those that call for a yes or no response, e.g., "Isn't that correct?" For your first twenty-five trials or questioning experiences, never ask an adverse witness an open-ended question. Make all your questions closed-ended in all critical areas.

In defense-witness psychiatrist Dr. Binger's testimony seeking to show accuser Whittaker Chambers was a pathological liar, referred to earlier, he stated that repetitive lying exemplified a psychopathic personality. In his cross-examination, prosecutor Murphy demonstrated the difficulty of defining the term *repetitive lying*. He structured his line of questioning by asking the doctor to define the term.

PROSECUTOR MURPHY: But doesn't repetitive lying mean, Doctor, a pattern of constant, repetitious lies without rhyme or reason? Isn't that what it means?

DR. BINGER: Not at all, not at all, if you will allow me to illustrate—

Q. [*refusing a digression*] If you would define it, it would help. Tell us what you mean by repetitive lying.

A. [*still trying to slip away*] I will give you one example of a patient—

Q. No. You tell us, please, if you can, what you mean by the phrase repetitive lying; define the term. Perhaps we don't understand each other.

A. [*again*] Will you let me exemplify it?

Q. No. I would rather have you define it.

A. I would have to say then "frequent lying."

As the preceding exchange shows us, Murphy successfully framed the questions to preclude Dr. Binger from expounding on his theory about psychopathic personality. This had a crucial twofold effect. By carefully limiting Dr. Binger's answers, Murphy succeeded in showing the difficulty of defining the exact meaning of the term, which was crucial to Dr. Binger's testimony. Second, by showing that Dr. Binger had difficulty in defining the term—repetitive lying—Murphy indirectly succeeded in planting the seeds of doubt in the jury's mind about the "expertise" of the doctor.

Film critics say that the genius of famed Swedish movie director Ingmar Bergman lies in his ability to let his audiences experience his film. He does not merely tell a story. Rather, he sets the stage and allows the events, the feelings, and emotions—including those of the audience—to interact.

The cross-examiner must remember that the jury is his audience. If the verdict goes against him, maybe it's because he has failed to present his story and its emotional overtones—his evidence—in a clear and interesting fashion. Most lawyers do not appreciate how to elicit information from witnesses in a manner that the ordinary person can understand. Too many do not know how to frame questions effectively. They fail to realize that the right question, at the right time, can have a devastating effect. Literally, the right question asked at the right time can make grown men cry. *Sixty Minutes* TV impresario Mike Wallace, I'm afraid, is better at doing this than most lawyers. Another nonlawyer in this fielding of questions is as sharp as a tack: author and interviewer on *Firing Line,* William F. Buckley, Jr.

In a federal case out on Long Island involving alleged political contributions of Hempstead town employees to the Republican party in order to get promotions and salary increases, a supervisor at the Department of Conservation and Waterways testified that she did not like to collect political contributions from her staff but was directed to do so by her immediate supervisor, the deputy commissioner of the Hempstead Department of Conservation and Waterways, Raymond Graber.

Mr. Graber testified that it was not his idea to collect campaign contributions, but he was ordered by his superior, the commissioner of the Hempstead Department of Conservation and Waterways to do so. In the middle of his testimony, the plaintiffs' attorney, Burt Neuborne, interrupted to throw a zinger question at Mr. Graber—"Did you ever lie under oath?"

At this point, Mr. Graber broke into tears. Neuborne then offered into evidence the fact that Graber had lied to a federal grand jury investigating similar charges and had been given a suspended sentence. The cross-examiner did not characterize Graber as a "liar" but rather sought to elicit dramatically the fact that he was a proven liar.

Many ask argumentative questions, which tend to confuse the listener and abuse the witness. Worse, such loaded questions never will rise to being acceptable evidence of any kind. Many other questioners sermonize, which make the jurors lose interest or retch.

Consider this example of characterizing a crucial question in an automobile personal liability suit:

Q. Mr. Witness, did you see the traffic light at the intersection of Main and Broad Streets seconds before the accident?

WITNESS: Yes.

Q. Could you tell us what the color of the light was from Main Street?

WITNESS: Green.

Assume that the witness had given a statement minutes after the accident to a police officer investigating the accident, saying the light was red. Cross-examiners sometimes take this unproductive tack:

Q. *Mr. Witness, you're lying!* You said on an earlier report that the light was red.

At this point the jurors could believe the questioner or not, because he was merely telling them the witness is lying. If the witness happens to be a sympathetic person, the jurors might believe the witness instead.

However, consider this as another approach:

Q. Mr. Witness, did you talk with a police officer immediately after the accident?
WITNESS: Yes.
Q. Did he ask you what the color of the light was from Main Street?
WITNESS: Yes.

You produce the police report and read the part where the witness stated the light was red. Human experience tells us that if a person says something contradictory he may be lying. What you have done is set the stage and then let the jury arrive at the conclusion that the witness is lying. Develop your evidence out of the witness's mouth, not your mouth.

* * *

A good example of how a cross-examiner handles sworn testimony considered sharply contradictory, if not false on one side, was the investigation of the Stirling Homex Corporation scandal. Four of its senior executives were convicted of stock frauds that mulcted investors of over $39 million. One witness in the case called by the government (with a financial interest in Stirling Homex Corporation) was lawyer–labor mediator Theodore W. Kheel, noted as a nemesis of Mayor Edward I. Koch. The other witness noted here was Lane Kirkland, then secretary-treasurer and now current president of the powerful AFL-CIO labor union.

To put it mildly, the testimonies at trial of Kheel and Kirkland squarely contradicted each other. The cross-examining prosecutor studiously avoided characterizing his questions. Rather, he meticulously and professionally honed his questions to nail down exactly what happened so there would be less chance of escape by facile explanation.

The prosecutor presented evidence that Stirling Homex was a highly promoted modular-home company. Theodore W. Kheel became a director, his law firm was retained as counsel, and he was given an option to buy two hundred thousand shares of Stirling Homex at a dollar each. The prosecutor alleged that the promoted stock soared to dizzying heights because Kheel had arranged a magnificent labor deal with the building trades unions previously reluctant to perform work on prefabricated housing. Theodore Kheel had made the labor pact arrangement with Lane Kirkland, the union leader. The prosecutor probed whether union leaders had received a payoff of any kind to clinch the sweet labor agreement.

Here are two contradictory excerpts from the transcript of the trial illustrating how the government prosecutor deftly handled questioning two of the witnesses, Theodore Kheel and Lane Kirkland:

PROSECUTOR: As to Lane Kirkland, did you arrange for any stock for him?

KHEEL: No.

Q. Did you ever prepare a promissory note for Lane Kirkland's signature in the amount of $58,300 for the purchase of stock in Homex?

A. I did not.

Q. Mr. Kheel, I show you Government's Exhibit 866 in evidence. . . . Did you prepare that note for his signature?

A. I did not.

Q. Is that envelope from your law firm?

A. It appears to be, yes. . . .

Q. Did you put Mr. Kirkland's name on the Homex [company] list to receive shares of Homex stock?

A. I did not.

Union leader Lane Kirkland was subpoenaed and called by the prosecutor as a rebuttal witness:

PROSECUTOR: Now, Mr. Kirkland, did you ever have a conversation with Theodore Kheel about your obtaining Stirling Homex stock?

KIRKLAND: Yes, sir.

Q. Could you tell us, please, where that conversation took place?

A. In Florida in February of 1970.

Q. Now, sir, could you please tell us . . . what Mr. Kheel said to you and what you said to him with regard to your acquisition of Homex stock?

A. As best I can reconstruct it . . . Mr. Kheel indicated to me that there would be a public issue of the stock of this company, that its prospects were very good, that it was in great demand, and that if I saw fit that he could probably arrange for me to secure some of the stock at the offering. I expressed interest, but subsequently . . . the issue arose—I think I raised it—that it might be best if I did not take it in the offering since that would appear to be a privileged or advantageous circumstance and position. I believe that he suggested to me that, if these reservations existed, that they could be avoided by placing an order for what I think is referred to as the second market, or when the stock became publicly available after the initial offering. I indicated that this sounded better to me and that I would be prepared to do it and asked him to make the arrangements on the assumption that it would be—the price would be within that range, three or four points.

Q. Did there come a time after these conversations, Mr. Kirkland, that you signed a document in Mr. Kheel's office?

A. I believe so, sir.

Q. Mr. Kirkland, I direct your attention to Government's Exhibit 866 in evidence. . . . I show you that, sir, and ask you if that is your signature?

A. I believe that is my signature. . . . I [have] a fragmentary memory of signing in Mr. Kheel's office a document which was a blank sort of note form of the type that this document appears to be. I do not have any recollection—I have no recollection of the entries on that document.

Q. Are you finished, sir?

A. I have a recollection of seeing Mr. Kheel two or three days later, at which point he told me that the stock exceeded the secondary market price. . . . Therefore, I was—none had been purchased on my behalf.

The prosecutor here exhibited wise restraint and fine technique. He did not characterize. He elicited evidence with clear, short questions. He was polite. He identified the critical government document by number for the record. There was little room to squeeze out. He neatly produced a direct confrontation. While the outcome of this contradiction was never legally resolved, it does provide for us an illustration of Maxim XXII.

MAXIM XXIII

Be Yourself

By the time you have tried your first case or had your first heart-pounding questioning experience, you have developed a certain personality, ways of expressing yourself, mannerisms, and habits of dress and movement. In my opinion the best course is to be yourself in court and not to try to imitate the personality, manner, or dress of someone else. Imitations of another person often create an insincere posture which may grate on the jury and the judge, or simply be ineffective.

At the opening statements of the so-called battle of the Titans on September 30, 1986, at the small, hundred-seat courthouse on the New Haven (Conn.) Green—the criminal prosecution of a covey of New York City officials and lawyers involved in the parking ticket collection scandal. Squaring off were Rudolph W. Giuliani for the prosecution versus Thomas P. Puccio for the defense. Giuliani led off in a serious manner: "This case is about the purchase and sale of public office." Giuliani closely followed a careful opening address to the jury, glancing down at loose-leaf notebooks. He did not wander from behind the podium. He was no-nonsense stern. He understood from extensive prosecution experience that juries seldom convict when the court atmosphere is jovial.

On the other hand, defense attorney Puccio was loose, relaxed, wisecracking, feeling free to talk seemingly off-the-cuff to the jury. He related some new sensational tidbits against key government witnesses he promised to prove. He joked about his adversary. Tensions in the courtroom relaxed. The lesson here is that both lawyers were being themselves in roles that had brought them each success.

The best-kept secret, Emory Buckner used to say, is that in some cases "annihilating" and "brilliant" cross-examination is open to the humblest if they are armed with the "right" letter, the "right" document or interview, the "right" record of conviction. You can glory in your success. "How many cases," he said, "are won or lost when the cross-examiner, skilled or unskilled, possesses a single piece of paper!" Be yourself and go for the evidence.

Despite your own state of development in the art of questioning, be true to your own self.

The Watergate hearings, ten years ago, are still remembered for bizarre revelations. Every day on television across the country, we experienced, as if actually present at the hearings, the ordeal of Watergate. It was perhaps one of America's national tragedies, testing faith in government and institutions of law.

It took a country lawyer to help reassure Americans that there were still people in Washington "with moral bearings solidly fixed," in *Time* magazine's phrase. Chairman Sam Ervin of the Senate Select Committee on

Presidential Campaign Activities used basic common sense. He offered pointed biblical allusions and *relevant* down-home anecdotes to steer his committee through the lies, muddled cover-ups, and conspiracies. Country lawyer Sam Ervin would sometimes drolly interject, "We could wind this up pretty soon if everyone would tell us what he knows, but if we continue to play hide-and-seek, then it could take a while."

We can hear the twang and see the twinkle.

The public audience *knew* we needed a show of frankness and common humanity, and many cheered as lawyer Senator Ervin scolded and questioned a cast of official witnesses. He was, during this dreadful time, a master of his craft.

MAXIM XXIV

Case the Courthouse Yourself and Arrive Early Every Day

There is no substitute for your own observation and absorption of the ambience *and* people at the courthouse. Before the trial commences, United States Attorney Lumbard taught sixty young assistants, take time to become familiar with the courthouse, the courtroom, and the court's personnel. Would you ever lecture in a hall you had not thoroughly cased ahead of time? Talk to the clerks. They know a lot. Visit around. During the trial, arrive at the courtroom well before the start of each day's session, giving the clear impression to all that you are prepared, organized, and eager to start the day's session. In the equity funding litigation, the great Wall Street scandal, the first hearing took place in Federal Court, Foley Square, attended by over three hundred lawyers. I arrived an hour early and found Judge Lee P. Gagliardi looking over arrangements for the onslaught of lawyers for the many parties. He named me liaison counsel for the defendants just because of being there early. You learn a great deal in the bargain. Listen.

MAXIM XXV

You Can Ask Why

When can you ask why on cross-examinations? Common advice is don't ever ask why in cross-examination. Such advice is based on four thousand years of experience, so don't knock it, but there are times when you can. Ned Carson's cross-examination of Oscar Wilde is a case in point—a criminal libel action brought against the Marquess of Queensberry, whose son, Lord Alfred Douglas, was apparently on intimate terms with Oscar Wilde.

Wilde instigated the criminal libel suit and thus brought ruin on himself. Queensberry had gone to Wilde's club and handed the porter a card on which he had written, "Oscar Wilde, posing as a sodomite." Wilde's response was to bring charges of criminal libel. The principal witness for the prosecution was of course Oscar Wilde, who relished the star role and brought the crowded courtroom into peals of laughter and hilarity by his clever put-downs of defense counsel Carson in the course of Carson's floundering cross-examination.

Carson had not neglected to investigate rumors of Oscar Wilde's amorous habits around London and had evidence that he consorted with grooms and bootblacks in curtained perfumed rooms. More likely this evidence would best have been presented through direct testimony, but his cross-examination of the Crown's principal witness had gone so badly that Carson decided he must use it there. Carson—taking a risk in replanning his sequence—inquired about a young man employed in a publishing house whom Wilde had taken to a hotel and given an elaborate dinner: "Was that for the purpose of having an intellectual treat?"

"Well, for him, yes," Wilde replied. The laughter in the courtroom was deafening. Carson plodded on.

He asked Wilde whether he knew that one of the men he entertained was a gentleman's valet and another a gentleman's groom. Wilde said yes. Carson then asked: "What enjoyment was it to you to be entertaining grooms and coachmen?"

WILDE: The pleasure of being with those who are young, bright, happy, careless, and original. [*more laughter*]

CARSON: Had they plenty of champagne?

WILDE: What gentleman would stint on his guest? [*rising laughter in the courtroom—for the last time*]

Carson, recovering, exclaimed, "What gentleman would stint the valet and the groom!"

Carson introduced the name of a young serving boy at Oxford. With a quick, jabbing thrust he asked Wilde, emphasizing each word, *"Did you ever kiss him?"* There was a sudden pause. The courtroom was quiet.

Wilde's simpering reply brought his downfall: "He was a particularly plain boy. He was unfortunately very ugly. I pitied him for it."

Wilde's answer left him completely exposed. "Did you ever kiss him?" was just the right question, had just the right timing, and created an opening for Carson to move in and deliver deadly blows. Carson asked Wilde over and over *why* he had referred to the serving boy's ugliness. *Why* had he said that the boy was particularly plain? Wilde was by the afternoon totally destroyed. The next day the Crown withdrew the prosecution for criminal libel against the Marquess of Queensberry. Later, Wilde was himself indicted, convicted, and sentenced to hard labor at Reading Gaol. His wife left him, and his children ignored him. Oscar Wilde, a man of tremendous brilliance, brought on the libel suit that induced his demise. He died alone and in poverty in Paris.

Cross-examination, preparation, genius, and luck led to the fall of ebullient Oscar Wilde. Until Wilde made his fatal answer, Carson would shun the open-ended question—the why—but once the adverse witness was impaled, inextricably, the flailing with the whys was safe and deadly.

You can also ask why if your pretrial discovery and other testimony has made you aware of facts that the opposing party simply cannot explain away. In this context the question why is rhetorical; the witness's silence speaks volumes to the jury.

* * *

During the late 1970s asbestos manufacturers and suppliers continued to be defendants in a large number of products liability cases. Asbestos workers in increasing numbers were filing claims for negligently allowing the workers to be exposed to harmful dust. The manufacturers' primary means of defense was, as referred to earlier, to claim that, at the time the workers were being exposed to the dust, no one knew that such exposure was harmful. The defendants used expert witnesses to testify that at the times in question there was a general lack of medical knowledge about the effects of exposure to asbestos dust. This defense was generally successful, until the diligent efforts of a few plaintiffs' attorneys made possible the successful cross-examination of these expert witnesses. Through the use of discovery, these attorneys uncovered detailed evidence that the asbestos industry had known for *decades* that asbestos dust could be deadly to people who worked with asbestos. With this information in hand, plaintiffs' attorneys were able to ask the defendants' expert witnesses the one question they could not answer: *Why hadn't the asbestos industry informed doctors and scientists about the evidence that asbestos dust could be harmful or deadly to workers?*

During the deposition of Dr. Richard Gaze, executive director of Cape Industries, Ltd., a major supplier of asbestos, it was disclosed that the asbestos industry had known about the dangers of asbestos dust. Scott Baldwin, one of the plaintiffs' lawyers, questioned Dr. Gaze. It was, according to one observer, "nothing short of masterly."

Q. Did you have any knowledge about the health hazards of asbestos?

A. Yes.

Q. When did you first know about it?

A. From the very first day I worked for Cape Industries in 1943.

Q. Did you ever inform any purchaser of asbestos, that it might be harmful to workers who used it?

A. As early as 1961 I had warned the directors of Pittsburgh Corning that asbestos could pose a very serious danger to their workers. He had discussed the problem at length with the officers of Pittsburgh Corning.

Q. Would it be accurate to say that you discussed this asbestos hazard with Pittsburgh Corning from 1961 down to about 1971?

A. Yes.

Q. Could you have ordered that warning labels be placed on the bags of asbestos being shipped from Cape Industries?

A. I could have recommended it.

Q. And you could have seen that it had been done, had you seen fit to do so?

A. Yes.

Concluding his questioning, Baldwin asked Dr. Gaze exactly what he knew about the dangers of asbestos. Dr. Gaze, who would die of mesothelioma at the age of sixty-five, answered with a bombshell that would effectively destroy the state-of-the-art defense which asbestos manufacturers had used successfully up to this point. Dr. Gaze then socked it to them in a summary answer. *"I knew that asbestos, improperly handled, could cause asbestosis, on breathing asbestos dust at too-high quantities for too long a time, could cause asbestosis. I have known this since the first day I was employed."*

Huge settlements have followed this adversarial breakthrough, the adroit use of the right questions.

MAXIM XXVI

The Meat-Hook Technique

Theodore Kiendl, a Columbia top athlete and superb trial lawyer, was known for the use of what I call the meat-hook technique. A masterful cross-examiner, Kiendl would invariably treat an adverse witness with the greatest courtesy and friendliness, making the witness less suspicious and more relaxed. Slowly, definitely, methodically, Kiendl developed evidence, question after question, until the witness was impaled on the meat hook by his own answers.

Then Kiendl would change in personality and flail the witness, sometimes rather harshly, for breach of trust, lack of good faith, petty dishonesty, insincerity, disloyalty, negligence, self-dealing, or offensive conduct—depending on the context. Often the jury, awakened to first-class theater, would be mesmerized, and the judge, brought from his reveries of retirement by a change of pace, would add (so there!) some telling questions of his own which finished off the sinking witness. The lesson is paramount in cross-examining your witness. Be certain your witness is hooked securely before you dramatize his naughty behavior.

MAXIM XXVII

Don't Gild the Lily

Once the adverse witness or his story has been discredited, don't hang in there with more questions; the witness might escape by explaining away his prior admissions. Be careful not to overstress, which would inadvertently give the witness an opportunity to qualify his answer or slyly place the matter in another context. You will have plenty of opportunities to emphasize the damaging admission or testimony in summation to the jury.

Observers insist that actress-patrician Alexandra Isles (who attended Chapin and Saint Timothy's schools with Sunny von Bülow) was the most dramatic witness at the first as well as the second von Bülow trial. Many believe her earlier testimony about incriminating admissions of her former lover had brought about his conviction on the first trial. She was hurt by the hostile reaction of von Bülow sympathizers and dreaded the prospect of going through the ordeal a second time after his conviction was overturned on technical grounds.

As the second trial approached, Alexandra Isles fled to Europe. Friends such as *New York* magazine critic John Simon stated she would never testify. She did not want to suffer on the witness stand as the former mistress of the accused, and worse, highlighted as the *motive* for the alleged attempted murder of Sunny. She was said to be "terrified" of being cross-examined by the formidable lawyer Thomas P. Puccio, who she thought would violate her most intimate privacy.

Ultimately she was induced to return in a dramatic flourish at the second trial. She testified on direct that von Bülow had telephoned her after Sunny's first coma to say that he had lain on the bed next to her for hours waiting for her to die. At the last moment he had simply not been able to go through with it, she testified, and then called the doctor.

At that moment von Bülow's lawyer, Thomas Puccio, rose to blast her damning testimony by pummeling cross-examination. The courtroom was electrified. Bringing himself to his full height, Thomas Puccio demanded that she explain to the jury how on earth she could have resumed a love affair with a man she suspected of trying to kill his wife. Alexandra Isles looked at Puccio for a moment, eyes fierce and unwavering. She replied, her voice staccato and rising, "Have you ever been in love?" The dreadful question back. Then she said to her devastated cross-examiner, *"I doubt it."* A hush fell over the courtroom as the significance of her barb sank in. Thomas Puccio had tried to gild the lily.

MAXIM XXVIII

Facts, Facts, Facts

In preparing for cross-examination in civil and criminal cases, J. Edward Lumbard placed strong emphasis on mastery of the facts. He would know the facts backwards and forwards before he began to cross-examine. Here was an appreciation of the phenomenon that cross-examination as opposed to direct examination of your own witness is the difference between slow-burning gunpowder and quick-flashing dynamite. Each does its work, but direct examination bursts along its marked line only, while cross-examination rends in all directions. Lumbard's cross-examination was more penetrating because he knew more facts than did the adverse witness. In his powerful summation, the facts, compelling and undeniable, were presented to the jury.

When he had drawn critical, devastating admissions of crucial facts in cross-examination, he would produce the trial transcript itself and read the words to the jury, line by line. The effect was irrefutable. In his first trial as United States attorney he prosecuted a vicious convicted criminal who had, in escaping from a surrounded Manhattan hotel, coldly killed an FBI agent with his pistol at the fire-escape-stair exit as the FBI agent was crouching, looking the other way through the lobby door. The critical issue was the intent of the defendant to kill. In twenty minutes prosecutor Lumbard gave the jury a litany of the defendant's evil intention to murder in order to escape from seizure by law officers—culled from the trial record. In ten minutes more, the jury brought in a verdict of guilty.

On the other hand, when the facts developed could not be viewed as airtight or overwhelming, J. Edward Lumbard would cross-examine on the *probabilities* based on normal common sense and experience. Lord Mansfield recognized the force of probabilities in one of his opinions: "As mathematical and absolute certainty is seldom to be attained in human affairs, reason requires that judges and all mankind in forming their opinion of the truth of facts should be regulated by the superior number of probabilities on the one side or the other."

There is no such thing as a computerized, robotlike, mechanized series of questions. All circumstances gather to illuminate the force of the cross-examination. The artful, radar-sensitive, and skilled touch makes the difference. As United States Attorney Emory Buckner passed on to his assistants in earlier days, "The young lawyer will learn the towering strength of *facts.* He will learn that consuming belief in his case is worth more than voice, and that contagious certainty as to its outcome is worth more than grace or a gesture."

Know the facts.

MAXIM **XXIX**

Avoid Beating Children, etc.

Do you remember the admonition, "Don't beat a child over the head in anger?" Well, never browbeat an old person, a woman, or a child. Be especially careful to treat courteously anyone who has little education, speaks with difficulty or with an accent, or has peculiar mannerisms. Jurors identify with the witness and will resent you, to the distress of your client's cause and yours.

Children present one of the greatest challenges to cross-examiner. Often the questioner must try to destroy the child's direct testimony; at the same time, he must not be too hostile or aggressive to the child. He must appreciate that children will always have the natural sympathy of juries. And yet he must not let this deter him from trying to get evidence of the truth from a child witness.

Here's a brief excerpt from the transcript of a recent child-abuse case, illustrating the delicate nature of questioning children under cross-examination. We see here how the cross-examiner was able to turn trouble around and evaporate the child's devastating earlier testimony without "beating her over the head."

DIRECT EXAMINATION

Q. [*by the prosecutor*] Did anybody ever hurt you when you were living in your real home?
A. Yes.
Q. What was that?
A. Spanking.
Q. Was there anything else?
A. Yes.
Q. What was the other thing?
A. Touched on the private parts.
Q. What are your private parts?
A. Crotch.
Q. Did anybody ever touch you, other than your crotch, in your private parts? Do you remember?
A. My butt.
Q. You said somebody touched you in your crotch with their finger; is that right or is that wrong?
A. Right.
Q. Did anybody tell you you should make those things up, that they weren't true?
A. No.
Q. Did they really happen then if you didn't make them up?
A. Yes.

* * *

CROSS-EXAMINATION

Q. [*by defense counsel*] Do you remember when Tom [a social worker] said, "Now it's time to practice for court . . . ?"
A. Yes.
Q. And you practiced saying "I'm telling you the truth" with Tom, didn't you?
A. Yes.
Q. And you practiced with Tom saying that your mom and dad touched you in the private parts, didn't you?
A. Yeah.
Q. And they kept telling you, "You have bad secrets," didn't they?
A. Yes.
Q. And before you were taken away from your real parents, you didn't have any bad secrets, did you?
A. Yeah.
Q. You told a lot of people it was just pretend, didn't you?
A. Yeah.
Q. And you kept telling them that nothing happened last year, didn't you?
A. Yes.
Q. But they wanted you to tell them that something happened, didn't they?
A. Yes.

Adults' questioning of children can be full of surprises and sometimes brings us unexpected amusement. However, any questioner, regardless of experience, should be on guard against what the child will say. U.S.

Education Director William J. Bennett recently took over a seventh-grade social studies class. He said he was "really nervous" about taking on twenty-seven twelve-year-olds. "When you go up to the [Capitol] Hill or hold a press conference you can anticipate the questions," he said. "Seventh graders can be *off the wall!*"

Myth and legend attribute extraordinary powers of prescience and truth to babes. I recall, out of the courtroom, a painter was doing a portrait in his studio of young Jeremy Rogers, seven-year-old son of an English canon of huge inherited wealth. While he was painting the young British heir, the following exchange took place, as written by Robert Harling in his lively novel, *The Summer Portrait:*

PAINTER: What's your best subject at school?
JEREMY: Scripture.
PAINTER: Why?
JEREMY: Because my father's good at it.
PAINTER: And next best?
JEREMY: Geography.
PAINTER: Give me the names of three English towns.
JEREMY: Camden Town.
PAINTER: That's not a town.
JEREMY: Why not? It says so.
PAINTER: I'm too busy to explain. Tell me another.
JEREMY: Kentish Town.
PAINTER: That's not a town, either.
JEREMY: Funny, it says so.
PAINTER: Do you do well at school?
JEREMY: So-so. I think it's best to be so-so—don't you?

PAINTER: Why?

JEREMY: Well, I've noticed if you're top you're always working to stay top, and if you're bottom they make you work jolly hard not to stay bottom. So-so chaps get along without all that.

PAINTER: You're seven, aren't you?

JEREMY: Next month I am. Twenty-two days to go.

PAINTER: You'll never say a truer thing, if you live to be eighty.

JEREMY: Oh, I don't know, it's obvious.

Fiction—novels, plays, movies—sometimes shows an apparent exception by exhibiting a rough, tough cross-examination of a woman. A case in point is the poignant movie, *Kramer vs Kramer.* Meryl Streep portrayed the woman, and Dustin Hoffman portrayed the man. The Kramers were married for eight years and had a little boy, Billy, seven years old. You recall that the wife left the husband and the child in New York and went to California. After two and a half years away, she sought to take custody of Billy from her now-divorced husband.

The custody suit came on for trial in gloomy ambience of Supreme Court, New York County. Mrs. Kramer's lawyer takes her through a ballet of direct examination. The judge is forbidding. Her lawyer turns her over to brutal, jugular cross-examination by an old hand. His cross is strategically compelling and dramatically brief. She ends the cross-examination in deep sobs and admission under oath that she had failed in the one most important relationship in her life: her marriage. After she finished (or was finished with), you remember that Dustin Hoffman whispered to his own lawyer, "Did you have to be so rough on her?" To which his lawyer hissed back: "Do you want the kid or don't you?" Pretty ice-cold stuff. Surprise. Verdict for the mother. Meryl Streep nonetheless gave Billy back to Dustin Hoffman. Everyone had a good cry.

But aren't we forced to ask whether even in fiction certain human principles prevail—abuse of a woman in cross-examination doesn't pay. She won the suit even from the gruff judge and with no jury to sympathize. The abused ex-wife chose to give custody of the boy to her former husband. Although fiction, the questions and answers are quite realistic and may in fact be based on a custody trial transcript.

The mood, the clashing thrusts, the tense interplay among counsel, witness, and judge, the footwork and the emotions all come out succinctly and dramatically in the movie scene of the direct and cross-examination of Mrs. Kramer. The stakes are high; the child's future is in equipoise: Will Mrs. Kramer survive the searing questioning by Mr. Kramer's brutally competent trial counsel? To see, feel, and hear this shattering episode, see the movie or lease the videotape cassette.

Here is a brief sample of Mr. Kramer's lawyer's flame-throwing cross-examination of Mrs. Kramer (*Kramer vs Kramer*, Columbia Pictures):

CROSS-EXAMINATION OF MRS. KRAMER

MR. KRAMER'S LAWYER: Now then, Mrs. Kramer, you say that you were married for eight years. Is that correct? [Closed-ended question.]

A. Yes.
Q. In all that time did your husband ever strike you or physically abuse you?
A. No.
Q. Did he ever strike or physically abuse his child?
A. No.
Q. Would you describe your husband as an alcoholic?
A. No.
Q. A heavy drinker?
A. No.
Q. Was he unfaithful?
A. No.
Q. Did he ever fail to provide for you in any way?
A. No.
Q. Hmmm . . . [*sarcastically*] Well, I can certainly see why you left him.

* * *

Q. Your Honor, I would like to ask what this model of stability and respectability has ever succeeded at. Were you a failure at the one most important personal relationship in your life?
A. It did not succeed.
Q. [*raising his voice*] Not *it*, Mrs. Kramer, *you!!* Were *you* a failure at the one most important relationship in your life? Were you?
A. [*long pause*] [*sobs*] [*nods*] [*long pause*].
Q. Is that a yes, Mrs. Kramer?
A. [*long pause*] [*sobs*] [*nods*] [*inaudible*]
Q. No further questions, Your Honor.

* * *

It is not unheard of that children can be used and abused by other than trial counsel, overstepping the bounds of fair play. Sometimes an unctuous judge can curry the jury's favor, indeed ignite it, toward overwhelming compassion for a child who, say, has suffered an (as yet unproven) injury in a terrible trolley car accident. How does the lawyer for the soulless defendant company treat the judge's fawning insouciance toward the child in front of a jury soon to be faced with determining the monetary damages from this deep-pocketed public utility.

In the particular case here, the defense counsel was the inimitable F. E. Smith, who was to become a famed barrister of strong mettle in the latter half of the nineteenth century, receiving the title Lord Birkenhead and serving as lord chancellor of England. His cohorts at the bar, equally dashing, were Edward Carson, Marshall Hall, and Rufus Isaacs. The young F. E. Smith was somewhat irreverent when he offered to defend the tramway company against the claim that as a result of the accident, the child (a boy) was apparently blinded.

The patronizing presiding officer was county court Judge Willis, who in his panelled courtroom in the presence of the jury began to rumble and mumble as if greatly moved by the boy's condition and fate.

"Poor, poor, poor, boy." [*head shaking with sadness*] "Poor boy. So he is blind in both eyes, I see. Poor boy!"

Then Judge Willis sharply said to his bailiff: "Put him up on a higher chair so the jury can see him."

Instantly, as if struck by a bolt of lightning, Smith was on his feet and, objecting solemnly, his inflection rising, he asked this question: "Perhaps Your Honor would like to have the boy passed around the jury box?"

Furious, Judge Willis shot back, "*That*, Mr. Smith, is a most improper question of the court. I will not allow it!"

Smith responded, "It was provoked, Judge Willis, provoked by a *most* improper suggestion."

There was a moment of angry silence before the judge said, "Counselor, have you ever heard of a saying by Bacon—the great Sir Francis Bacon—that youth and discretion are ill-wed companions?"

"Indeed, I have," Smith quickly replied. "And has Your Honor ever heard of a saying by Bacon—the great Bacon—that a much-talking judge is like an ill-tuned cymbal?"

Judge Willis sputtered pompously, "You are inexcusably offensive, young man."

At which point F. E. Smith added, "As a matter of fact, we both are; the only difference between us is that I am trying to be, and you can't help it."

MAXIM XXX

When You Have Made Your Point, Sit Down!

During cross-examination or public questioning out of court always look for a high-peak chance to terminate and sit down.

As the old master cross-examiner Max Steuer put it, "When you have scored your point on cross-examination, for heaven's sake, quit."

INDEX

ABOUT THE AUTHOR

The author, Peter Megargee Brown, lives in New York City with his wife, Alexandra Stoddard, an interior designer and writer, and family. He graduated from Yale College, class of 1944; Yale Law School, 1948; he is a past president, Federal Bar Council; special assistant New York State attorney general and assistant counsel, New York State Crime Commission, 1951–53, under John Marshall Harlan; assistant United States attorney in charge of the Federal Waterfront Prosecution, 1953–56 under Judge J. Edward Lumbard; former partner and head of litigation, Cadwalader, Wickersham & Taft. He is a Fellow, American College of Trial Lawyers. Mr. Brown practices law in New York City.